Woodworking

Techniques, Tips, and Projects from a Master Craftsman

To my father,
William Edgar Bigelow
who never locked his tools from his clumsy sons.
We miss him.

Woodworking

Techniques, Tips, and Projects from a Master Craftsman

B. William Bigelow

TAB | TAB BOOKS
Blue Ridge Summit, PA

FIRST EDITION
FIRST PRINTING

Copyright © 1989 by TAB BOOKS
Printed in the United States of America

Library of Congress Cataloging-in-Publication Data

Bigelow, William (William B.)
Woodworking techniques, tips, and projects from a master / by
William Bigelow.
p.   cm.
ISBN 0-8306-9255-X :   —ISBN 0-8306-3255-7 (pbk.) :
1. Woodwork.   2. Woodworking tools.   3. Power tools.   I. Title.
TT180.B54   1990
684'.08—dc20   89-29164
                                                              CIP

TAB BOOKS offers software for
sale. For information and a catalog,
please contact TAB Software Department,
Blue Ridge Summit, PA 17294-0850.

Questions regarding the content of this book
should be addressed to:

Reader Inquiry Branch
TAB BOOKS
Blue Ridge Summit, PA 17294-0214

Acquisitions Editor: Kimberly Tabor
Book Editor: Cherie R. Blazer
Production: Katherine Brown

Contents

Acknowledgments

I wish to thank, only as a son and husband can, Reta and Maureen Bigelow, whose faith in my personal ability and enthusiastic encouragement of this project never flagged. Maureen also contributed projects—Jewelry Box, Coffee Grinder, Dough Tray, Curved Treasure Chest, Piggy Bank, and Round Birdhouse—in addition to hours of word processing. My friend John Nelson is largely responsible for this book through a well-placed bet, which I lost. He is the draftsman behind each project. Deborah Porter's photographic talent is evident throughout the book. Special thanks to the students of Conval Regional High School, who not only endorsed the work with fresh ideas, but became the guinea pigs of each new chapter.

Introduction

This book is about machine woodworking techniques. It is written for the intermediate woodworker, and illustrates methods of using woodworking machines to your best advantage. The book also contains 25 fully illustrated projects, each developed to practice the techniques introduced.

When developing this book, I decided to discard any pretext of being comprehensive. There is such a multitude of skills and interests in the woodworking field that no one book can include them all. Techniques here are geared to intermediate woodworking skills and deal with the basic woodworking machines found in the home workshop: table saw, band saw, router, drill press, belt and disk sander, and wood lathe.

Included with the woodworking techniques are projects, complete with plans and directions. Projects plans are given so that the reader may immediately find a use for each new technique. Often we read about a new technique, only to file it away, hoping it will be of use someday. Many times the new idea is forgotten before it is used. Because I have developed popular project plans that are especially designed to use all the techniques demonstrated, each technique may be explored right away.

It is suggested that the novices purchase this as their second or third book, rather than the first. There are many fine books available that explore basic machine operations, hand tool selection and use, layout, and finishing skills. Basic machine woodworking skills, such as how to safely crosscut or rip wood on the table saw, have been left out of this book. Likewise, there are no illustrations on band saw contour cutting, or router setup. Two chapters, however, have been included on table saw and band saw tune-up. These chapters are included because many of the techniques both on the band saw and table saw depend on correct machine setup.

Safety

Each reader should be familiar with the basic safe use of the table saw, band saw, router, drill press, disk sander, and wood lathe. Space limitations, as well as the intent of the book, preclude lengthy discussions on how to operate these machines. For example, readers should have safe operating experience concerning crosscutting and ripping stock on the table saw before attempting a cove cut or box joint on this machine. All photos and instructions on machine techniques are supportive of good safety practices, such as the use of safety guards whenever possible. *Safety guards are sometimes pulled back for clear photos*, but this is only an illustrative necessity and *not suggested* for common practice. Knowing and practicing safety makes woodworking an enjoyable hobby, and perhaps for some a rewarding occupation.

I

Table Saw Techniques

THE FOLLOWING INFORMATION ON THE TABLE SAW INCLUDES FIVE TECH-
niques and eight project ideas. The table saw (Fig. I-1) is used to cut box
joints, raised panel doors, compound miter joints, cove cuts, and the jerry joint.
Because of space limitations, only a table saw setup check is included in the text;
basic table saw introduction, setup, and ripping and crosscutting are omitted.
Many fine books are available that cover basic safe machine use, and these
should be read by the beginner before the techniques in this book are attempted.
The intermediate techniques presented here are not difficult, and expand the use-
fulness of the table saw in the workshop.

The table saw will be at its best when it is tuned to run smooth and true. Like
a car, the table saw runs gradually out of tune, slowly enough that the lack of
accuracy and performance is not immediately noticeable. Check your saw and
bring it back in tune before attempting these projects.

1. The saw should run smooth. If it vibrates, disconnect the power and
   look for the source. If the problem is a bent motor shaft, worn motor

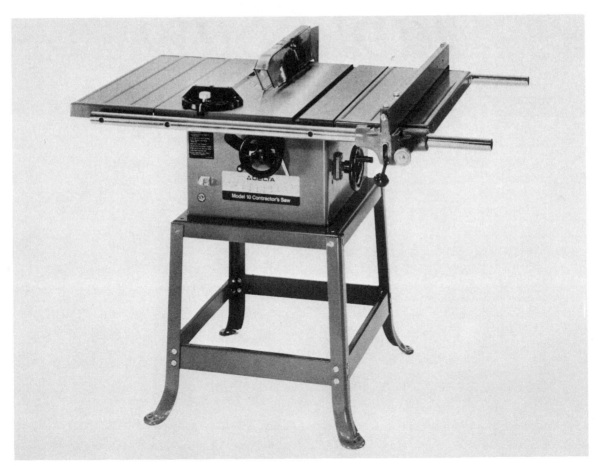

Fig. I-1. The table saw (Courtesy Delta).

bearings, wobbly pulleys, worn belt, bad blade or arbor bearings, find the source and correct before going further.

2. Install a sharp blade. With the power disconnected, raise the blade to maximum height. Wiggle the blade from left to right. There should be no play in the arbor bearings. Lower the blade, connect power, and turn the saw on. The blade should be balanced and run true.

3. Level the throat plate with the table (Fig. I-2). A level throat plate will keep stock from bumping up or down as the wood is passed over the plate and through the blade.

4. Check that the miter slots are absolutely parallel to the blade. This is the most overlooked trouble area. Disconnect the power and raise the blade up to maximum height. Mark one tooth that is set to the left. Swing that tooth to the front of the table, at table height, and measure the exact distance from the tooth to the miter slot on the left. This can be done with a combination square.

   Put the head of the combination square in the miter slot and set the blade to the tooth (Fig. I-3). Lock the blade height in place. Swing the marked tooth to the back of the saw, at table height (Fig. I-4). Check this distance with the combination square; it must be exactly the same as

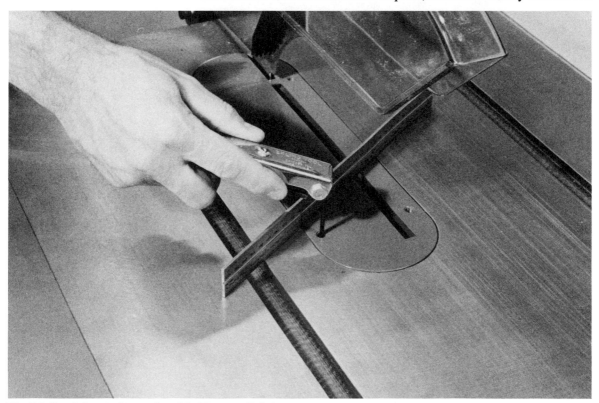

Fig. I-2. Level throat plate to the table (Courtesy Delta).

Fig. I-3. Check the distance from a marked tooth to the miter slot (Courtesy Delta).

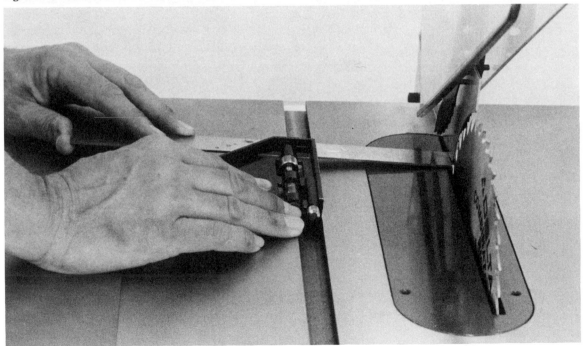

Fig. I-4. Swing the marked tooth to the back and recheck distance to the miter slot (Courtesy Delta).

Fig. I-5. Adjust fence parallel to the miter slot (Courtesy Delta).

the front measurement. This is the time to be fussy. If the two measurements are not exactly equal, the table saw must be adjusted before moving on. The tables on most of heavier machines are bolted on with three or four bolts. These bolts may be loosened and the table shifted to bring the blade (arbor) parallel with the miter slot. For some owners, it might be necessary to dig out the owners manual to correct the machine.

5. While the blade is cranked up and the power disconnected, check that the blade is 90 degrees to the table surface. Use an accurate square for this. Adjust the blade to 90 degrees, then check the tilting arbor pointer, or stop screw. Adjust if necessary.

6. Slide the miter gauge into its slot and adjust the miter gauge with a square so that it is 90 degrees to the blade. Adjust the pointer or the stop on the miter gauge if necessary.

7. Check that the fence is parallel to the blade (Fig. I-5). Slide the fence over to the edge of the miter slot and clamp down. The miter slot is now parallel to the blade and may be used to adjust the fence.

1
Box Joints

BOX JOINTS ARE STRONG, ATTRACTIVE CORNER JOINTS. A LARGE SIDE GRAIN with a glue area make the box joint among the strongest corner joints. If visible end grain is not objectional, the box joint is a good choice.

Box joints may be cut on the table saw with a two-piece wooden indexing jig and dado cutters. The jig is designed to hold the stock safely and index the cuts so the fingers of the joint slip nicely together. The process illustrated will cut and space the fingers of the joint the same thickness as the boards to be joined. Stock that is 1/2-inch will have 1/2-inch-square fingers; 3/4-stock will have fingers 3/4 square. After the directions are understood, it is possible to alter the finger size by altering the blade width, indexing pin size and location respectively.

Step One: Screw a flat plywood piece to the miter gauge. It must be wide enough to clamp the stock securely above the dado blade and long enough to support the stock along its entire width, plus a few inches. Next check the table saw setup. See the checklist. A few checks will eliminate wondering what went wrong later (Fig. 1-1).

Step Two: Adjust dado blade *width* to equal the thickness of the stock. Now to make the index jig: Adjust the blade height to be slightly *lower* than the stock thickness. This will ensure good chip clearance when the box joint is cut. A plywood table insert fitting close to the blade is an excellent idea (Fig. 1-2).

Step Three: Cut through the plywood board (Fig. 1-3).

Step Four: Make and insert an index "pin" the same thickness as the stock being cut and the width of the blade (Fig. 1-4).

Fig. 1-1. Box joints: Step 1.

Fig. 1-2. Box joints: Step 2.

Fig. 1-3. Box joints: Step 3.

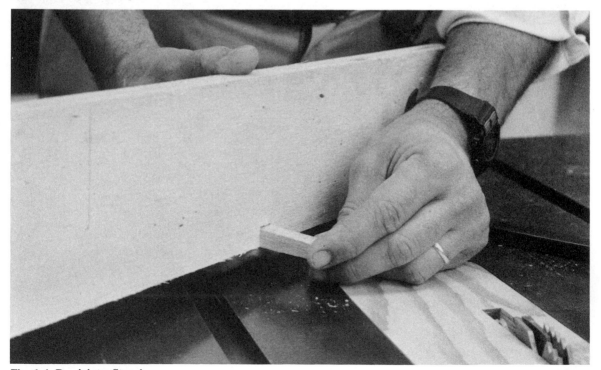

Fig. 1-4. Box joints: Step 4.

Step Five: Unscrew the plywood jig from the miter gauge and shift the board to one side of the blade as shown. Gauge the new location from a spacer block of stock being used. Resecure the plywood to the miter gauge. Now the width of the blade, the spacer width, and the index pin width will be the same (Fig. 1-5).

Step Six: Raise the blade height slightly higher than the stock width. This will run the box joint fingers slightly above the finished joint for end grain sanding later (Fig. 1-6).

Step Seven: Mark and clamp part A against the index pin as shown. Use a clamp. It will be safer, and provide a cleaner cut by holding the stock firmly against the plywood jig. The photo shows the first cut completed (Fig. 1-7).

Step Eight: Continue cutting across part A, placing the previous cut on the index pin. Keep the table saw surface clean so that the stock does not ride up on the sawdust (Fig. 1-8).

Step Nine: The mating part (B) is cut next. Mark the starting point as shown (Fig. 1-9).

Step Ten: Clamp part B for the first cut (Fig. 1-10).

Step Eleven: Part B is now finished (Fig. 1-11).

Fig. 1-5. Box joints: Step 5.

Fig. 1-6. Box joints: Step 6.

Fig. 1-7. Box joints: Step 7.

Fig. 1-8. Box joints: Step 8.

Fig. 1-9. Box joints: Step 9.

Fig. 1-10. Box joints: Step 10.

This completes the box joint. Once the process is understood the joint size can be modified, as long as the width of the dado blade, space, and index pin respectively remain the same. In the example, 1/2-inch-thick stock was used and the finished box joint fingers were 1/2-inch square. Since the stock was 5 1/2 inches wide, the box joints came out even on the far end of the cut (Fig. 1-12). Thicker stock could be used with this same setup, provided the blade height be adjusted to accommodate the change in stock thickness. Blade height would be adjusted slightly higher than the stock thickness in all cases.

With 1/2-inch stock, the box joint fingers will come out even (full fingers), provided the width of the stock is in some even multiple of 1/2 inch. Whatever the width of the stock, the fingers will come out full, in the end, if the dado blade, space, and the index pin are set in some even multiple of the width of the stock selected.

I often use box joints in drawer construction and have multiple A and B parts. In this case, clearly mark the outside and top of each part to avoid having parts that are mismatched around the drawer. The top edge of each joint is cut first. On the first drawer (or box) a little experimentation is in order, before all the parts are machined. A little time with scrap stock can spare you many mistakes.

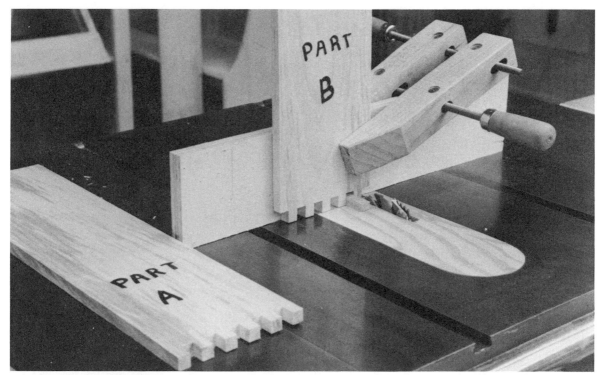

Fig. 1-11. Box joints: Step 11.

Fig. 1-12. Completed box joints: Step 12.

Project 1: Treasure Chest

What young lady wouldn't love to stow away her diary or treasured necklaces and charms from someone special in this box-jointed treasure chest? This is not the giant hope chest of the future, but a small $5^1/4$-$\times$-10-inch storage for smaller treasures (Fig. 1-13).

Order the hinges, hasp, and bails before starting the project. The Woodworkers' Store, 21801 Industrial Boulevard, Rogers, MN 55374-9514, is the outlet that supplied the hardware pictured on our chest. The order numbers are on the blueprints.

Choose a wood that does not splinter for this project. When making box joints, splintering can occur with some woods. Good woods include walnut, cherry, birch, maple, apple, and perhaps cedar (Table 1-1).

The chest is made as a complete box. The lid is sawn off after the sides, top, and bottom are glued up (Fig. 1-14).

Resaw the wood to the $1/4$-inch dimension of the plans. Cut the top and bottom of the box $5^1/4 \times 10$ inches long, the front and back 4×10 inches, the two ends are $4 \times 5^1/4$ inches. Follow the box joint technique on the front and back, and two end pieces. Cut the feet from $1/2$-inch stock using the band saw for the curve of the design (Fig. 1-15).

Fig. 1-13. Treasure chest.

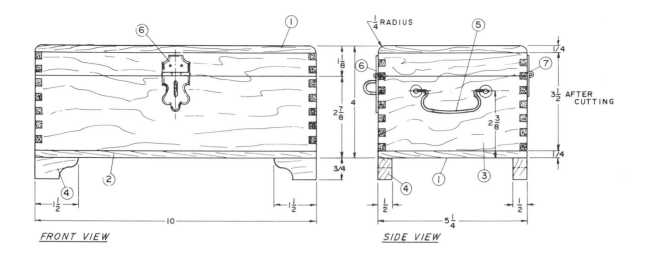

FRONT VIEW

SIDE VIEW

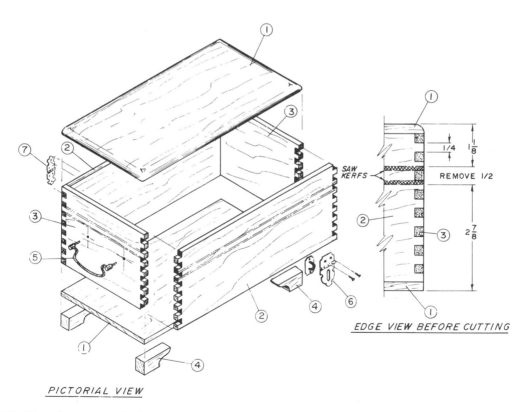

PICTORIAL VIEW

EDGE VIEW BEFORE CUTTING

Fig. 1-14. Plans for treasure chest.

Table 1-1. Materials List: Treasure Chest.

NO.	NAME	SIZE	REQ'D.
I	TOP / BOTTOM	1/4 X 5 1/4 - 10 LONG	2
2	FRONT/ BACK	1/4 X 4 - 10 LONG	2
3	END	1/4 X 4 - 5 1/4 LONG	2
4	FOOT	1/2 X 3/4 - 1 1/2 LG.	4
5	BAIL 2 1/2" SIZE	E 1804	I PR.
6	HASP	D1265	I
7	HINGE	D1267	I PR.

Glue the joints up, clamp with strap clamps, and check that the corners are square. When dry, measure and align the top and bottom to the open box. Glue into place.

Sand the box before the lid is cut off. Sand all the box joints as well as the top and bottom, flush with the sides.

The lid is sawn off after the box is made. It is sawn twice (note the saw kerfs in the drafted plans), removing a 1/2-inch section. One complete set of box joints are missing so that the others will line up accordingly (Fig. 1-16).

Fig. 1-15. Resaw parts to 1/4 inch.

Fig. 1-16. Saw the lid off.

Sand the sawmarks off the lid and box. Place sandpaper on a flat surface and move the box across the sandpaper to keep the edges flat (Fig. 1-17). Align and glue the feet to the bottom of the chest.

Stain the chest and lid. If you wish to leave the inside of the chest unstained, you could line it with fabric or rich velvet.

Locate and mark the hardware placement, then apply all hardware. A tiny lock and key can add a personal touch.

Fig. 1-17. Sand the lid joint on a flat surface.

Project 2: Coffee Grinder

The anticipation of smelling that good ground bean fragrance will make this simple coffee grinder an enjoyable project. You will probably have admirers asking where you found your grinder. Besides, you get to practice the box joint technique (Fig. 1-18).

It is best to order the grinder casting first and check the casting against the size shown in the plans. Begin by cutting up stock for the parts listed in the bill of materials. Many species of wood will work, but be sure the wood is not toxic or allergenic (Table 1-2).

The drawer parts not seen—the sides, back, and bottom—can be made of secondary wood such as pine or poplar. If practical, try resawing the parts from thicker stock. This will allow you to economize on wood and acquire some practice resawing.

The drawer front is cut from the front side, so saw all sides the same size first, then rip the drawer front off the front side panel. Rip with a narrow kerf (a band saw blade works fine) so that the drawer front will have about a $1/16$-inch clearance (Fig. 1-19).

Fig. 1-18. Coffee grinder.

Table 1-2. Materials List: Coffee Grinder.

NO.	NAME	SIZE	REQ'D.
1	COFFEE MILL	F1130*	1
2	BACK	1/4 X 4 3/4 - 5 LONG	1
3	SIDE	1/4 X 4 3/4 - 5 LONG	2
4	FRONT	1/4 X 1 3/4 - 5 LONG	1
5	BOTTOM	1/4 X 5 1/4 - 5 1/2 LG.	1
6	DRAWER-FRONT	3/8 X 3 - 5 LONG	1
7	DRAWER-SIDES	1/4 X 3 - 4 3/8 LG.	2
8	DRAWER-BACK	1/4 X 3.- 4 1/8 LG.	1
9	DRAWER-BOTTOM	1/8 X 4 1/8 - 4 1/4 LG.	1
10	DRAWER PULL	1/2 DIA. - 3/4 LONG	1
11	FOOT PAD	1/2 DIA. (FELT)	4

*Woodworker's Supply of New Mexico.

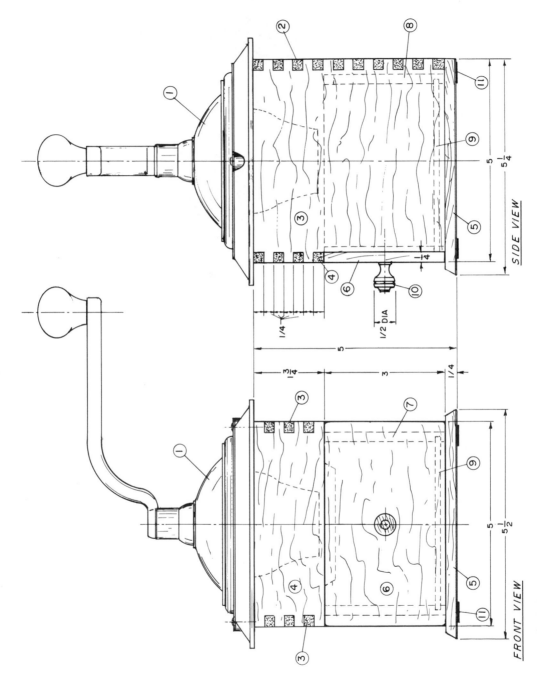

Fig. 1-19. Plans for coffee grinder: Front and side views.

Next, lay out and cut the corner box joints. If using a splintery wood, try taping both sides of the end being cut with masking tape. Tape $1/4$ inch up from the bottom; this will keep splinters from lifting as the box joints are cut. Remove the tape immediately after the joint is cut.

Trial fit the sides (parts 2, 3, and 4). Then cut the lower box joints of the sides, as shown, to accommodate the drawer front. When satisfied with the box joints, glue the sides. A beefy elastic or strap clamps work well for this. Use two tongue depressors at each corner, which will evenly distribute the clamping force close to the box joint. Check for squareness before the sides are set aside to dry (Fig. 1-20).

While the sides dry, make the drawer. Fit the drawer bottom, beveled thin at the edges, in a groove on all four sides. Leave a slight expansion space in the drawer back so that the drawer bottom can expand across its grain. The back of the drawer (part 8) is notched at the top to clear the coffee grinder casting. Glue the drawer sides around the bottom. Do not glue the bottom grooves.

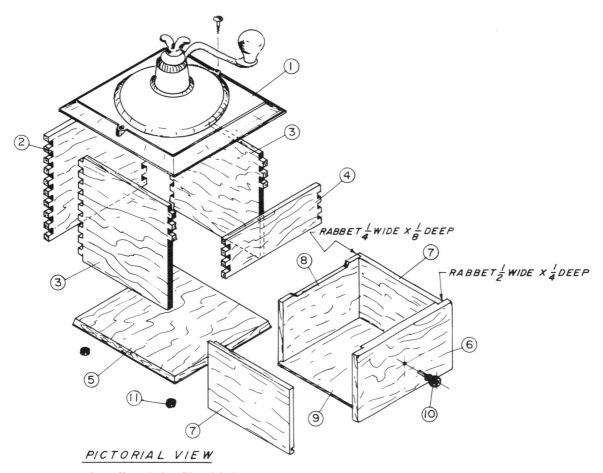

PICTORIAL VIEW

Fig. 1-20. Plans for coffee grinder: Pictorial view.

21

The 1/2-inch drawer pull is turned on the lathe, then centered and screwed in from inside of the drawer front. If a lathe is not accessible, use a small purchased knob.

Cut the bottom (part 5) and bevel the edges. Sand the box joints flush, before the sides and bottom are joined. Then center the side assembly on the bottom, glue and clamp in place.

Apply the finish before the grinder casting is screwed in place. A non-toxic finish is required for this project; the coffee grinder illustrated here was oiled with a salad bowl finish. The drawer inside may be left unfinished. Also, paraffin wax can be applied to the outside of the drawer sides so it will slide out easily upon your first try.

Secure the casting with two screws from the top. Place the beans, which can be purchased from your local market, in the casting, and enjoy your new coffee grinder.

Raised Panels

The table saw is a versatile machine that will cut a variety of panel doors. Each door may be as individual as the maker. Although I do make panel doors with the shaper and door cutters, nine times out of ten, I choose the table saw technique, especially for better projects. The shaper produces smooth work with molding profiles that fit beautifully together. Why choose the table saw rather than the shaper? Shaper cutters are very expensive, and dressing like an astronaut for protection against the dust and the high speed whine of the shaper is not much fun. And this method results in doors like the ones purchased at the factory. I save the high-speed cutters for production runs, and reserve the table saw for individual work.

Project 3: Raised Panel Doors

The earliest cabinet makers soon discovered that board doors with boards fashioned edge to edge just did not remain stable (Fig. 1-21). Board doors are heavy and change size with seasonal changes of humidity. They swell and stick in humidity, and become much too loose in dry weather.

Panel doors are made of a frame and one or more panels. The frame consists of vertical stiles and horizontal rails. Panel doors have the grain of the frame running around the perimeter of the door. This makes a stable door, because wood expands and contracts very little along the grain (Fig. 1-22).

Another advantage of the panel door is its lightness. The frame can support a light panel and still be quite sturdy. The frame is made to hold the panel while allowing for movement caused by temperature or humidity. Door panels are made of wood, glass, plastic, metal, and other materials. The panel is supported by the door frame and does not add to the structural integrity of the door. The information given here is limited to smaller cabinet wood panel doors, although the techniques will be useful in constructing any panel door.

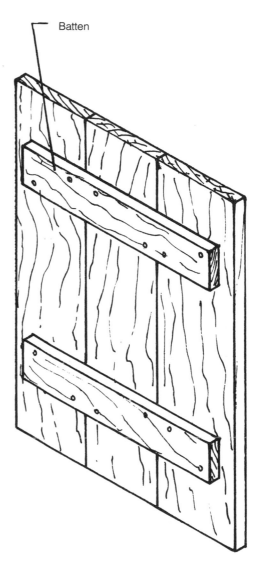

Batten

Fig. 1-21. A board door.

Consider what the door will be like upon completion. Plan the overall size, thickness of the frame, width of stiles and rails, and type of wood. Decide upon the size of the panel, and its thickness, and whether it will be flat, raised, or have designs such as carving. An imaginative panel makes a distinctive door. A sketch is almost always out of proportion, so draw full size or in scale to check relative size of the door parts to themselves and to the cabinet or furniture piece. Remember: Table saw techniques are so variable that rails, stiles, and panels may be very different from door to door. Generally the bevel in a raised panel is about half the width of the stile, and the rails tend to be the heavier members of the frame. Often the bottom rail is the wide member of the frame (Fig. 1-23).

Start construction by gluing up the panel if stock on hand is not wide enough. The panel will "float" in grooves in the frame, so make sure the panel

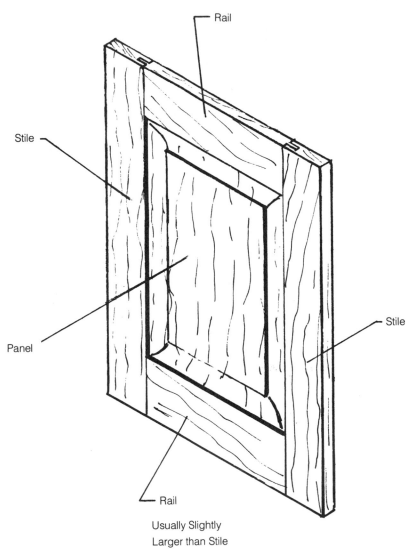

Rail

Stile

Stile

Panel

Rail

Usually Slightly
Larger than Stile

Fig. 1-22. A panel door.

size is larger than the opening. If the panel is to be thin, a board can sometimes be resawn and bookmatched for the best grain pattern. Don't hesitate to mix woods for different effects. Plane extra scrap stock when fabricating panels the same thickness, then use the scrap later to test cuts on the table saw.

The frame rails and stiles are usually connected together with mortise-and-tenon joints. The rails are cut with a tenon and the stiles are mortised. In small doors, the mortise may be open and relatively shallow, merely an extension of the panel groove in the stile (Fig. 1-24A). In heavier doors, the rail tenon should be deeper into the stile, with the joint pegged after assembly. These mortise-and-

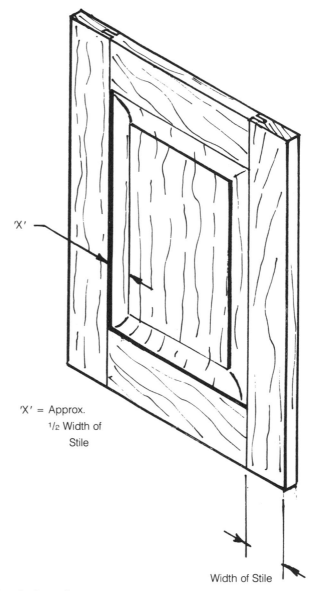

'X'

'X' = Approx.
1/2 Width of
Stile

Width of Stile

Fig. 1-23. Detail of a raised panel.

tenon joints hold the door frame together and the tenon is sized according to the weight of the door.

If a haunched tenon is used (Fig. 1-24B), the panel groove may be ripped to the end of the stile. Later the mortise for the tenon may be cut deeper. This method differs from the light door (open mortise) only in that the tenon is cut longer and haunched. The mortise, as stated, is chiseled deeper for the haunched part of the tenon after the table saw work is done.

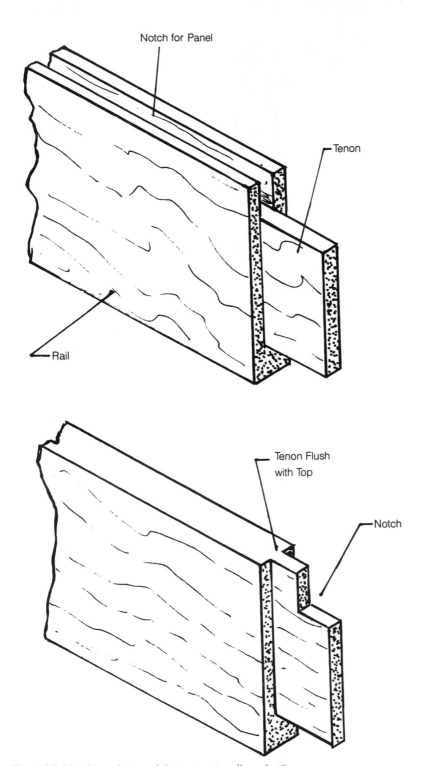

Notch for Panel

Tenon

Rail

Tenon Flush
with Top

Notch

Fig. 1-24. Mortise-and-tenon joint connects rails and stiles.

After the door size has been planed, rip and crosscut the stiles and rails to required size. Be sure to cut the rails long enough for the tenons. Lay out the frame and mark the inside edges for the panel groove. The directions that follow apply to a small door. Here the tenon will be cut as deep as the panel groove.

Cut the panel groove the length of the rails and stiles. Cut against the table saw fence, with a $^1/_4$-inch dado setup (Fig. 1-25). Then cut the tenons in the rails. Although Fig. 1-26 shows the tenon cut horizontally using multiple cuts with a fence stop, they may be cut vertically with a tenon jig.

Dry fit the frame and measure the panel size. How big should the panel be? How much should it float in the groove? I allow at least $^3/_{16}$ inch expansive and contractive clearance per foot across the grain of the panel. To answer these questions more exactly, the following must be considered:

- The moisture content of the panel and frame.
- The type of wood and how it was sawn from the tree.
- The environment in which the door will be used.
- The average humidity or season of the year in which the door is made.
- The width of the panel across the grain.

Remember that the door frame is relatively stable, the grain runs around the perimeter, and movement with the grain is slight. Therefore, the door frame stays

Fig. 1-25. The panel groove is cut in the rails and stiles with a dado blade.

27

Fig. 1-26. The tenons are cut horizontally.

Fig. 1-27. Two-step panel of spalted birch.

the same size from season to season. The panel does not. The big movement is not along the length (with the grain) of the panel, but across the panel width. Wood swells and shrinks quite a bit across the grain as it takes on and releases water from the air, so allow for this in the grooves at the side of the panel. If you need to know more, refer to Bruce Hoadley's *Understanding Wood* (Taunton Press). It is an excellent book for the cabinetmaker.

Figure 1-27 shows a two-step raised panel of spaulted birch, with several decorative cuts. (Panel has been cut thick for photo clarity.) The bevel is cut with the panel vertical and against the fence. Notice the bevel is not cut to the surface of the panel (Fig. 1-28). After the bevel cuts are made, the panel will be cut again to make a step. If a step is not desired, the saw blade may be raised to cut the finished bevel in one step.

Experiment with the tilt of the blade starting at 10 degrees, and adjust more or less until the desired bevel is reached. A higher blade adjustment with a tilt less than 10 degrees will cut a long bevel. The edge of the panel should fit the groove in the stile (Fig. 1-29). A simple jig is needed to maintain accuracy and to keep the panel from sliding down the throat plate—which is dangerous. Complicated jigs may be constructed, but a board clamped to the panel that rides on the fence will do the job. The panel should be kept against the fence by a feather board (Fig. 1-30). Make test cuts on scrap wood that is the same thickness as the

Fig. 1-28. The bevel is cut in the panel.

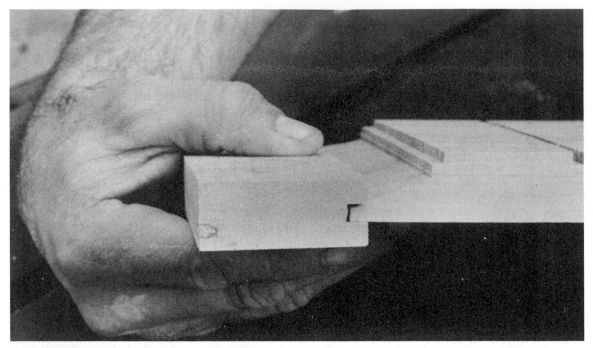

Fig. 1-29. The edge of the panel fits rail/stile groove.

Fig. 1-30. Bevel cut in the end grain of the panel (Note: the feather board and simple fence jig. Guard has been pulled back for viewing purposes).

Fig. 1-31. The safe way to cut bevels.

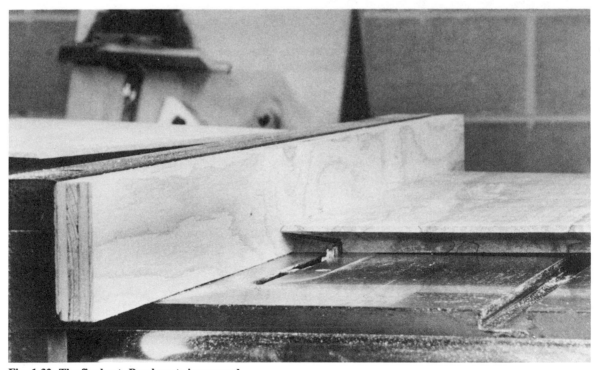

Fig. 1-32. The final cut. Panel waste is removed.

Fig. 1-33. Bonnet hutch.

panel (Fig. 1-31). A sharp blade will keep investment in sandpaper and labor to a minimum, because saw and burn marks from a dull blade or a fence not parallel with the blade are a chore to remove.

Once the bevel cuts are finished, adjust the saw blade back to 90 degrees and adjust the blade height and fence to cut out the bevel (Fig. 1-32). It is a good safety practice to stand to the side of the saw during this cut; the beveled section that has been cut free might come sliding back.

Sand and finish the panel before it is assembled in the frame. Glue only the frame parts together during assembly. Remember that the panel should be free to expand and contract across the grain, and finishing material should not clog up the grooves in the panels. Large panels are usually pinned in the center top and bottom, through the rail. This will keep expansion and contraction of the panel centered in the frame.

Project 4: Bonnet Hutch

This pine hutch is wonderful for any home (Fig. 1-33). It is quite narrow at 19 inches, and so will fit many handy locations. The hutch has panel doors, top and bottom, to store a host of things inside. This one has been painted and antiqued, but it also looks good stained and finished in natural wood (Table 1-3).

Table 1-3. Materials List: Bonnet Hutch.

NO.	NAME	SIZE	REQ'D.
1	SIDE	3/4 X 8 3/4 -72 LONG	2
2	SHELF-TOP	3/4 X 8 -18 LONG	7
3	BACK-BOARD	3/4 X 9 1/4 -72 LONG	2
4	STILE-TOP	3/4 X 2 1/4 -42 LONG	2
5	STILE-BOTTOM	3/4 X 2 1/4 - 29 1/4 LG.	2
6	TOP RAIL	3/4 X 2 1/4 -14 1/2 LG.	1
7	TOP-FRONT	3/8 X 4 - 22 3/4 LG.	1
8	TOP-SIDE	3/8 X 4 - 11 3/8 LG.	2
9	MOLDING-CUT TO FIT	3/4 X 7/8 -60 LONG	1
10	SHELF-FRONT	3/4 X 1 3/4 - 21 LG.	1
11	SHELF-END	3/4 X 1 1/4 X 8 3/4 LG	2
12	DOOR STOP TOP	3/4 X 3 - 17 1/2 LG.	1
13	DOOR STOP BOTTOM	3/4 X 1 - 17 1/2 LONG	1
14	HINGE	1 1/2 X 2 SIZE	4
15	DOOR PULL	7/8 DIA. X 2 1/2 LG.	2
16	DOOR LOCK	1/2 X 3/4 - 2 1/2 LG.	2
17	DOOR STILE	3/4 X 2 1/8 - 39 3/4 LG.	2
18	DOOR RAIL	3/4 X 2 1/2 - 11 1/4	5
19	DOOR PANEL	1/2 X 11 - 16 7/8 LG.	2
20	DOOR STILE	3/4 X 2 1/8 - 27 LONG	2
21	DOOR PANEL	1/2 X 11 - 25 7/8 LG.	1

If the hutch is to be painted or made to look old, there are several steps along the way that will simplify the final finishing work, as well as make the piece appear more authentic. First, hand plane all parts before they are assembled. Use a hand plane with a convex ground blade, so that the surface will be scalloped in shallow waves. This will telescope through the paint and duplicate old work. Remove all planer and jointer marks; they will also telescope through the paint and ruin the antique effect. Second, use square nails and leave them flush with the surface.

The hutch is not much more difficult than a bookcase to build. This piece actually is a bookcase, with face frame and panel doors added to the front (Figs. 1-34, 1-35).

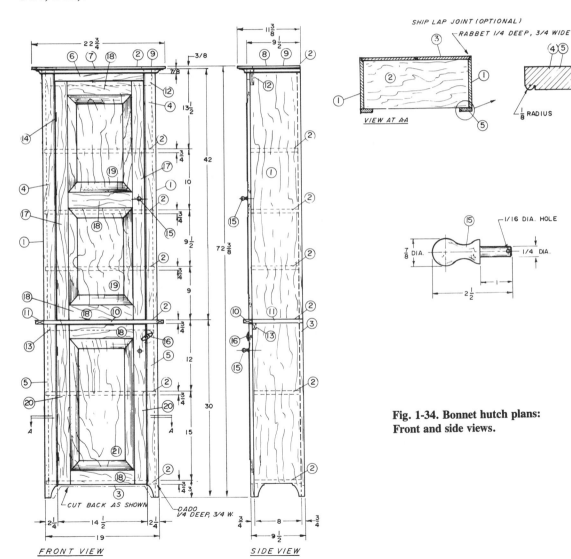

Fig. 1-34. Bonnet hutch plans: Front and side views.

Make the case first, add the face frame, then make the doors to fit the opening. This is a good project to practice using the router double fence jig and the panel door technique.

Start by ripping and crosscutting the end boards and all the shelves to size, as listed in the bill of materials. Sand or plane smooth all surfaces before doing any further work on the hutch. Then lay out the shelf dado locations and cut the dados with a router and the double router fence. Rip the rabbet in the end boards (part 1) to house the back panels on the table saw. Lay out and cut the opening at the bottom of the end boards with a saber saw. Be sure to stay below the bottom shelf. The case is now ready to be nailed or glued up.

Trial fit the shelves, then glue and nail the case together. Align the shelves flush with the front. If the end boards are cupped, use bar clamps and blocks to draw the end boards flat. Carefully square the case before leaving the glue to set (Fig. 1-34).

Fig. 1-34. Bonnet hutch plans: Foot detail.

Next, cut the back board to fit the rabbet groove in the case. If the back board is of solid wood, it will shrink and swell with temperature changes, so accommodations must be made for this movement. There are two ways to do this: Make the back panel from two boards, shiplapped or splined in the middle without glue, so that movement can occur in these joints. Or, if the back is one board, allow for movement in the rabbet joint with the end boards.

If you choose the second alternative, nail the back board to the shelves, but do not nail or glue the rabbet joint between the end board and back panel. If the wood is good and dry—8 percent moisture content or less—and it is in the dry season, leave a gap for expansion. The gap should be about 1/4 inch total. Conversely, if the wood is swollen and the humidity is high, the gaps may be small, allowing for shrinkage later. When the back panel is sized correctly, nail it to the case into the shelves (Fig. 1-36).

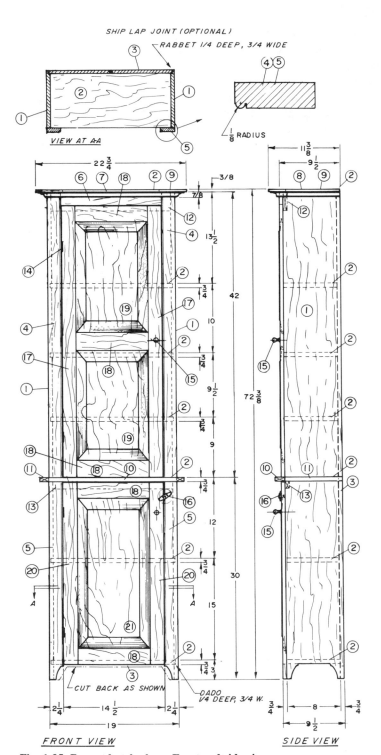

Fig. 1-35. Bonnet hutch plans: Front and side views.

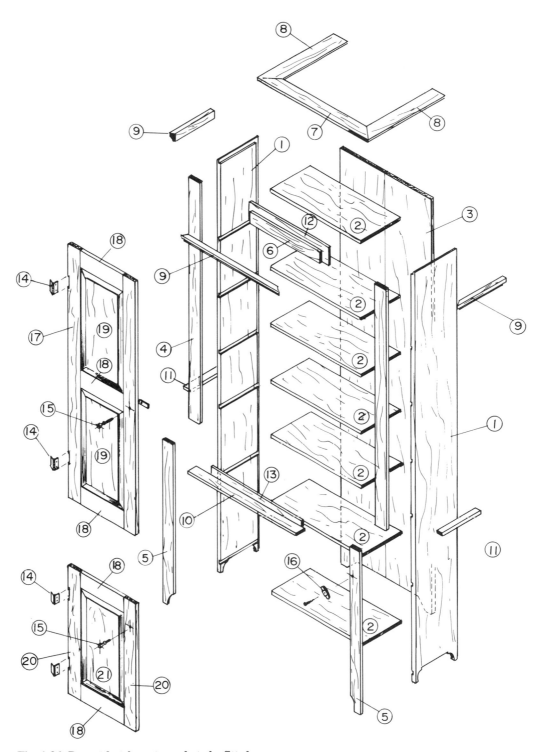

Fig. 1-36. Bonnet hutch parts ready to be fitted.

Turn the case over and install the face frame (parts 4, 5, 6, 10). The face frame stiles (parts 4, 5) have a beaded groove machined in the front inside of each piece. Then add the shelf ends (part 11) and the door stops (parts 12, 13). Cut and install parts (parts 8, 9), and the case is complete.

The doors are built last to fit the openings. Study the panel door technique described previously, then mortise in the hinges and fit the door. Finally, locate and drill for the knob and latch assembly.

The hutch is ready to be finished. The following techniques apply to the painted hutch in the photo, which was painted, repainted, and distressed to appear old. First, the hutch was stained on the inside and back, then painted on the outside, except for the back toward the wall. It is not necessary to use paint where it does not show. The first layer of paint on the outside was red, the second layer was colonial grey blue. The second layer is the finished background layer of the chest.

After the second layer of paint dried, the hutch was worn and distressed. Bumps, scrapes, and worn spots mark the exterior. Part of the front ledge, the knobs, and surrounding area were sanded down to bare wood to simulate years of handling. Sanding exposes (feathers out) the first layer of paint, contrasting with the second coat. The bare wood exposed looked new, so it was darkened later. The piece was distressed in areas likely to be damaged with the passage of time, while other areas, such as the top, were left alone. The hutch was sanded and stained on the inside at the front top edge of the shelves and the back where dishes might have leaned. You may even add simulated jar ring stains to the lower shelves by coating the bottom of several size jars with stains, paint, or even coffee, and placing them on the shelves.

The piece was darkened to simulate age with a mixture of $1/2$ part oil base flat black and $1/2$ part paint thinner. This mixture was applied, then immediately wiped off. You can do this to all parts of the hutch, inside and out. The mixture darkens any raw wood exposed to sanding, and tones down the fresh paint. Black paint lodges in the low spots, such as the scratches and bumps, accenting those areas.

At this stage decorative painting was added. A top coat of sealer was added to protect the paint, and then the piece was waxed.

2

Compound Miters and Bevels

THE NEXT FOUR PROJECTS—THE CLOCK, CANDY DISH, WOODEN BUCKET, AND stave canister—make use of the table saw with the saw arbor tilted. The clock uses a tilted arbor (22¹/₂ degrees) with the miter gauge set at 90 degrees. The candy dish uses a compound miter where the saw arbor and the miter gauge are set at angles other than 90 degrees. The wooden bucket combines the tilted saw arbor with a taper jig (beveled tapered staves). The canister uses the table saw to rip wood at a bevel.

Two handy tables are included. Table 2-1 lists the arbor setting and miter gauge angles for compound miters. Table 2-2 refers to stave angles. With these tables, the size of all three projects could be changed and many new projects designed.

Project 5: Octagonal Clock

A home can never have enough clocks, especially handmade by the owner. Take a few evenings of shop work and add this one to your den or family room. Cherry was chosen for the clock, but many woods would be equally attractive (Fig. 2-1).

This octagonal wall clock is a good way to practice edge miter on the table saw. The small clock uses a minimum of wood, and can be cut out with a table saw, router, and saber or jigsaw.

Order clock parts before you start. This clock is sized for the dial face, hands, and quartz movement listed on the bill of materials. The size of the clock

Table 2-1. Settings for Compound Miters.

NUMBER OF SIDES	ANGLE BETWEEN SIDES	SETTINGS	FLAT JOINTS → 90°	85°	80°	75°	70°	65°	60°	55°	50°	45°	40°	35°	30°	25°	20°	15°	10°	5°	→ ON-EDGE JOINTS 0°
4	45°	TILT SAW	0°	4°	8°	11.5°	15.5°	19°	22.5°	26°	29°	32°	35°	37°	39°	41°	42.5°	43.5°	44.5°	45°	45°
		MITER	45°	45°	44.5°	43.5°	42.5°	41°	39°	37°	35°	32°	29°	26°	22.5°	19°	15.5°	11.5°	8°	4°	0°
6	30°	TILT SAW	0°	2.5°	5°	8°	10°	12.5°	15°	17°	19°	21°	23°	24.5°	26°	27°	28°	29°	29.5°	30°	30°
		MITER	30°	30°	29.5°	29°	28°	27°	26°	24.5°	23°	21°	19°	17°	15°	12.5°	10°	8°	5°	2.5°	0°
8	22½°	TILT SAW	0°	2°	4°	6°	7.5°	9.5°	11°	13°	14.5°	16°	17°	18.5°	19.5°	20.5°	21°	22°	22°	22.5°	22.5°
		MITER	22.5°	22.5°	22°	22°	21°	20.5°	19.5°	18.5°	17°	16°	14.5°	13°	11°	9.5°	7.5°	6°	4°	2°	0°
10	18°	TILT SAW	0°	1.5°	3°	4.6°	6°	7.5°	9°	10°	11.5°	13°	14°	15°	15.5°	16°	17°	17°	17.5°	18°	18°
		MITER	18°	18°	17.5°	17°	17°	16°	15.5°	15°	14°	13°	11.5°	10°	9°	7.5°	6°	4.6°	3°	1.5°	0°
12	15°	TILT SAW	0°	1.5°	2.5°	4°	5°	6.5°	7.5°	8.5°	9.5°	10.5°	11.5°	12.5°	13°	13.5°	14°	14.5°	14.5°	15°	15°
		MITER	15°	15°	14.5°	14.5°	14°	13.5°	13°	12.5°	11.5°	10.5°	9.5°	8.5°	7.5°	6.5°	5°	4°	2.5°	1.5°	0°
15	12°	TILT SAW	0°	1°	2°	3°	4°	5°	6°	7°	8°	8.5°	9°	10°	10.5°	11°	11.5°	11.5°	11.5°	12°	12°
		MITER	12°	12°	11.5°	11.5°	11.5°	11°	10.5°	10°	9°	8.5°	8°	7°	6°	5°	4°	3°	2°	1°	0°
18	10°	TILT SAW	0°	1°	2°	2.5°	3.5°	4°	5°	6°	6.5°	7°	7.5°	8°	8.5°	9°	9.5°	9.5°	9.5°	10°	10°
		MITER	10°	10°	9.5°	9.5°	9.5°	9°	8.5°	8°	7.5°	7°	6.5°	6°	5°	4°	3.5°	2.5°	2°	1°	0°

ALL FIGURES ARE ROUNDED OFF TO THE NEAREST .5° (1/2")

ANGLE OF SLOPE (SIDES)

MITER SETTINGS FROM 90°

3/4 THICK MATERIAL

EXAMPLE

Table 2-2. Settings for Stave Angles.

EXAMPLE

NUMBER OF SIDES	BLADE TILT SETTING	MAX. OUTSIDE DIAMETER	MIN. INSIDE DIAMETER	MAX. WALL THICKNESS	STAVE WIDTH
6	30°	3	1 7/8	9/16	1 3/4
		3 1/2	2 3/8		2 11/16
		4	3	1/2	2 5/16
		4 1/2	3 1/4		2 5/8
		5	4 1/8	7/16	2 7/8
		5 1/2	4 5/8		3 3/16
		6	5 1/4	3/8	3 1/2
8	22 1/2°	3	1 3/4	5/8	1 1/4
		3 1/2	2 1/4		1 3/8
		4	2 3/4		1 11/16
		4 1/2	3 3/8	9/16	1 7/8
		5	3 7/8		2 1/8
		5 1/2	4 3/8		2 5/16
		6	5		2 9/16
		6 1/2	5 1/2	1/2	2 5/8
		7	6		2 7/8
10	18°	3	1 3/4		15/16
		3 1/2	2 1/4		1 1/8
		4	2 3/4		1 1/4
		4 1/2	3 1/4	5/8	1 3/8
		5	3 3/4		1 9/16
		5 1/2	4 1/4		1 11/16
		6	4 7/8		1 13/16
		6 1/2	5 3/8	9/16	2
		7	5 7/8		2 3/16
12	15°	3	1 1/2	3/4	13/16
		3 1/2	2 1/8		15/16
		4	2 5/8		1 1/8
		4 1/2	3 1/8	11/16	1 1/4
		5	3 5/8		1 5/16
		5 1/2	4 1/8		1 1/2
		6	4 3/4		1 5/8
		6 1/2	5 1/4		1 3/4
		7	5 3/4	5/8	1 7/8
		7 1/2	6 1/4		2
		8	6 3/4		2 1/8
15	12°	4	2 5/8		7/8
		4 1/2	3 1/8		15/16
		5	3 5/8		1 1/16
		5 1/2	4 1/8		1 3/16
		6	4 5/8	11/16	1 5/16
		6 1/2	5 1/8		1 3/8
		7	5 5/8		1 1/2
		7 1/2	6 1/8		1 9/16
		8	6 5/8		1 3/4

EXAMPLE

SAW BLADE TILT ANGLE

STANDARD 3/4 THICK

STAVE WIDTH

WALL THICKNESS

Table 2-2. Continued.

		8 1/2	7 1/8		1 13/16
		9	7 5/8		1 7/8
18	10°	4	2 5/8		3/4
		4 1/2	3 1/8		13/16
		5	3 5/8		7/8
		5 1/2	4 1/8		1
		6	4 5/8		1 1/16
		6 1/2	5 1/8	11/16	1 1/8
		7	5 5/8		1 1/4
		7 1/2	6 1/8		1 5/16
		8	6 5/8		1 7/16
		8 1/2	7 1/8		1 1/2
		9	7 5/8		1 9/16
20	9°	5	3 3/8		13/16
		5 1/2	4 1/8		7/8
		6	4 5/8		1
		6 1/2	5 1/8		1 1/16
		7	5 5/8		1 1/8
		7 1/2	6 1/8	11/16	1 3/16
		8	6 5/8		1 1/4
		8 1/2	7 1/8		1 3/8
		9	7 5/8		1 7/16
		9 1/2	8 1/8		1 1/2
		10	8 5/8		1 9/16
24	$7\frac{1}{2}$°	6	4 5/8		13/16
		6 1/2	5 1/8		7/8
		7	5 5/8		15/16
		7 1/2	6 1/8		1
		8	6 5/8		1 1/16
		8 1/2	7 1/8	11/16	1 1/8
		9	7 5/8		1 3/16
		9 1/2	8 1/8		1 1/4
		10	8 5/8		1 5/16
		10 1/2	9 1/8		1 3/8
		11	9 5/8		1 7/16

ALL DIMENSIONS ARE ROUNDED TO THE NEAREST 1/16 INCH

may be easily modified for different faces, hands, and movement. To change the size, draw a full-size octagonal layout for the new face board. From the new layout, the sides of the octagon may be measured and parts on the bill of materials changed accordingly. Once modified, make sure the clock is deep enough for the movement you have purchased (Table 2-3).

Start by machining a 1/2- × -2- × -48-inch strip for the sides of the clock. If each side is sequentially cut from this strip, the grain will "wrap" around the clock. Any favorite wood will do for the clock, even a mixture of woods. Try laminating the side strip with stripes, or cut the face board from interesting woods—including spaulted, bird's-eye, or sapwood/hardwood combinations (Fig. 2-2).

Before the edge miters are cut from the strip, machine a wide rabbet in the back of the strip, and a 1/2-inch dado (plow) to hold the face frame. The rabbet

Fig. 2-1. Octagonal clock.

Table 2-3. Materials List: Octagonal Clock.

NO.	NAME	SIZE	REQ'D.
I	FRAME	1/2 X 2 - 5 1/2 LG.	8
2	FACE BOARD	1/2 X 12 3/8 X 12 3/8	I
3	DIAL SUPPORT	1/4 X 12 3/8 X 12 3/8	I
4	GLASS	9 3/4 DIA.	I
5	GLAZING	—	—
6	DIAL SUPPORT BACK	1/4 SQ. - 48" LG.	I
7	DIAL FACE 8"DIA	NO. R-800	I
8	MOVEMENT	NO. P 559-X	I
9	HANDS 4" SIZE	INCLUDED	I PR.

will house the dial support. Cut the rabbet and dado with a dado head on the table saw (using hold-down feather boards), or cut them with the horizontal router (Fig. 2-3).

Now cut the side miters from the strip. The sides must each be exactly 5½

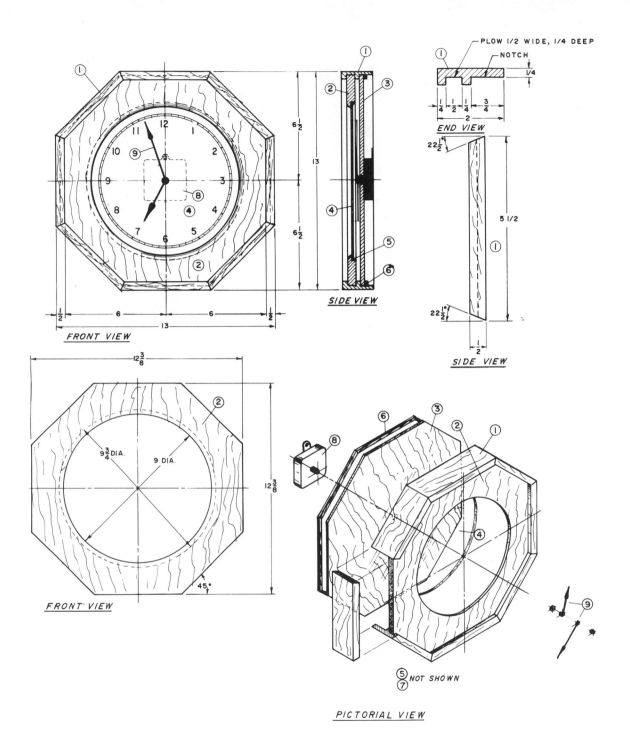

PLOW 1/2 WIDE, 1/4 DEEP

NOTCH

END VIEW

SIDE VIEW

SIDE VIEW

FRONT VIEW

FRONT VIEW

9¾ DIA.

9 DIA.

45°

PICTORIAL VIEW

NOT SHOWN

Fig. 2-2. Octagonal clock plans.

44

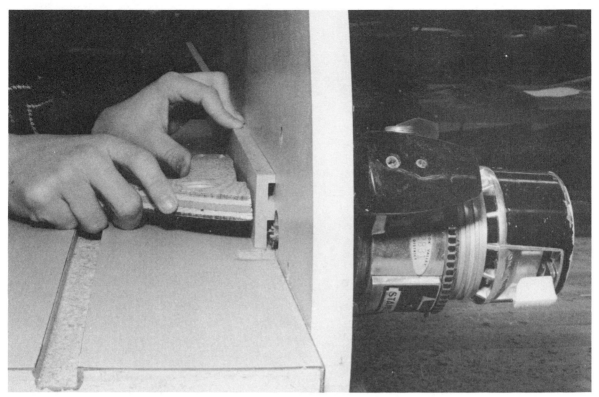

Fig. 2-3. The clock dado and rabbet are cut with the horizontal router.

inches long, with each end mitered 22^1/$_2$ degrees. The table saw must be set up accurately for these cuts. Check the miter gauge against the table saw blade. (Do this with power disconnected, saw blade 90 degrees, arbor pointer at zero.) Lock the miter gauge 90 degrees to the blade, then crank the table saw arbor to 22^1/$_2$ degrees. Figure 2-4 shows the first cut on the end of the strip. *Note*: The guard is pulled back for photo clarity. Figure 2-5 shows one side of the clock trimmed. One clamp secures a stop block on the miter gauge, and the second holds the short side section during the cut.

Dry fit the sides together with a strap clamp. Arrange the sides so the grain flows around the clock. Number each piece so the clock may be reassembled in the same order when the clock is glued up around the face board.

Before the strap clamp is removed, use this assembly as a pattern to mark the face board. Set the side assembly down on the face board with the rabbet (back of the clock) down. The rabbet and the dado are cut to the same depth so that the rabbet may be used to mark the face board. Set the grain direction in the face board, in harmony with the side octagon, then mark by running a pencil around the inside of the rabbet. Mark one side of the face octagonal with the corresponding side so it may be relocated the same way later. In similar manner, mark the dial support.

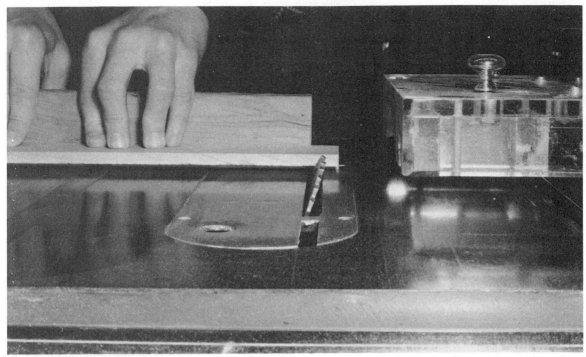

Fig. 2-4. First cut at 22¹/₂ degrees.

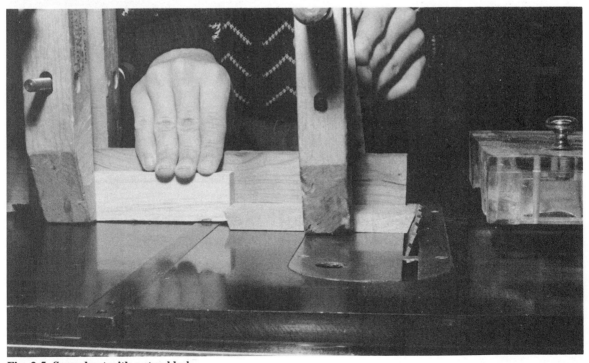

Fig. 2-5. Second cut with a stop block.

Next, locate the center of the dial face in the face frame. Draw a circle from the center for the dial. Cut the circle out, rout the outside with a $1/4$-inch radius, and rabbet the inside for the glass. Drill a hole in the circle area, and cut out the circle with a saber, jig, or coping saw (Fig. 2-6). Carefully sand down to the compass line. A drum sander on the drill press is a good way to do this. The inside edge of the circle needs to be smooth because the router bearing will ride on this surface, and any bumps will spoil the $1/4$-inch radius on the edge of the cutout.

Use a $1/4$-inch router bit with bearing first to cut the outside radius (Fig. 2-7). Then switch to a wing cutter for the inside rabbet (Fig. 2-8). If a wing cutter is not available, a mortising bit may be used to rout the rabbet, provided that the router is guided by an outside jig.

Cut out the octagonal pattern in the face board. Sand the face board so that it will fit a little loosely in the clock dado groove. If it fits slightly loose before it is glued in, it will expand and contract a bit with the seasons and not crack. Sand the front of the face frame before assembly.

Glue up the side miters and strap clamp the assembly around the face frame. Glue only the miters. Check that each miter is aligned correctly, and each side placed in sequence before putting aside to dry (Fig. 2-9).

Fig. 2-6. The clock circle is cut with a saber saw.

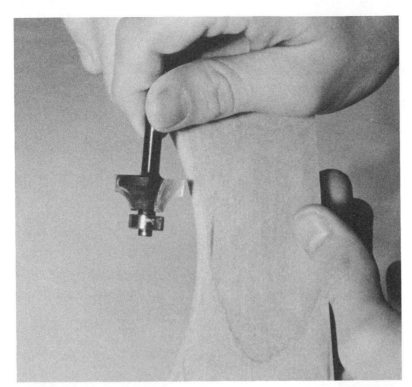

Fig. 2-7. The outside of the hole is rounded with a ¼-inch radius.

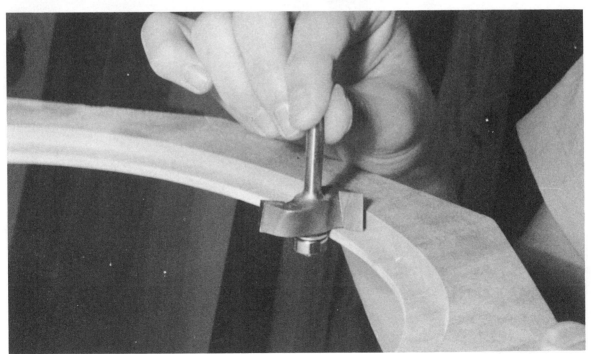

Fig. 2-8. Use a wing cutter for the inside radius.

48

Fig. 2-9. Glue and strap clamp the sides around the face frame.

While the glue dries, mount the dial face on the dial support board. Drill a hole in the clock face for the movement, mount the clock, and attach the hands. The glass is cut in a circle and mounted with standard window points and glazing in the face board. Cut the glass slightly undersize so it is a little loose in the face board. This will allow the face board to shrink without cracking in dry weather. Sand the outside of the clock and apply a finish.

Project 6: Small Canister

This small canister is made from staves glued together into a cylinder (Fig. 2-10). More simple than a bucket or a barrel, these staves are straight with beveled edges. The parts are glued together to form a straight-sided cylinder.

Techniques for both staves and round cylinders may be used for canisters. The difference in construction is apparent in the finished grain in the canister walls. The band-sawn cylinders show a pattern tangent to the growth rings, much like a veneer peeled from a rotating log. Often insect damage shows on the surface. There is only one glued seam in the canister's wall. The stave canister, on the other hand, will show different grain in each individual part. Staves may be arranged and rearranged for different effects. The number of staves used and the

Fig. 2-10. Stave canister.

Table 2-4. Materials List: Stave Canister.

NO.	NAME	SIZE	REQ'D.
1	SIDE (STAVE)	3/4 X 1 5/8 – 5 LONG	12
2	BOTTOM	3/4 X 5 1/8 DIAMETER	1
3	LID -- GLUE UP............	5/8 X 5 1/4 DIAMETER	1
		5/8 X 2 7/8 DIAMETER	1
		5/8 X 1 5/8 DIAMETER	1

STAVE DETAILS
   6" OUTSIDE DIAMETER
   1 5/8 STAVE WIDTH
   SAW BLADE TILT = 15°
   5/8 WALL THICKNESS

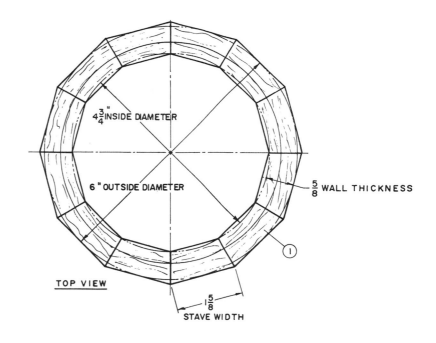

4 3/4" INSIDE DIAMETER

6 " OUTSIDE DIAMETER

5/8 WALL THICKNESS

①

TOP VIEW

1 5/8 STAVE WIDTH

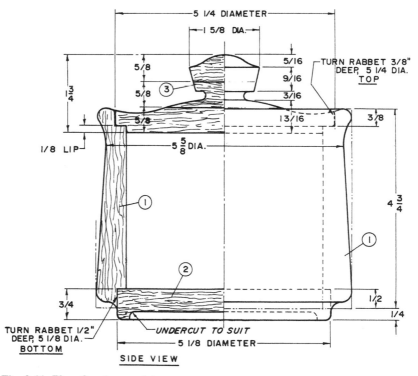

5 1/4 DIAMETER

1 5/8 DIA.

5/16

TURN RABBET 3/8" DEEP, 5 1/4 DIA.
TOP

5/8

9/16

5/8 ③

3/16

1 3/4

13/16

3/8

1/8 LIP

5/8

5 5/8 DIA.

①

4 3/4

2

①

3/4

1/2

1/4

TURN RABBET 1/2" DEEP, 5 1/8 DIA.
BOTTOM

UNDERCUT TO SUIT

5 1/8 DIAMETER

SIDE VIEW

Fig. 2-11. Plans for stave canister.

height and diameter of the cylinder can be varied for different canister sizes (Table 2-4).

The stave canister illustrated here has 12 sides (Fig. 2-11). The staves are cut by tilting the table saw arbor to 15 degrees, and ripping the staves against the table saw fence. Ideally, long stock is ripped with the bevel on both sides, then crosscut to length. Practically, however, short pieces are fished out of the scrap pile and used first (Fig. 2-12).

Ripping short pieces on the table saw will be both safe and accurate if a few precautions are followed: Take a few moments to check the table saw setup. Can the fence be set positively parallel to the blade? Is the blade stiff, sharp, and running true? And finally, is the throat plate flat and level with the surface?

Throat plates are too often overlooked and can be warped, or set too high or low. At worst, the small pieces for the canister will bump up or down over the throat plate, possibly changing direction over a warped throat plate. This kind of action will ruin the accuracy of the bevel joint as well as invite a nasty kickback. The wood should slide past a flat fence on a smooth and flat table surface. A push stick is a must. Good control and smooth action will eliminate fussing with the bevels later, and allowing everything to fit.

After the staves are beveled and cut to length, the 12-sided cylinder may be fitted and glued. Lay the staves on the bench with the outside of each stave up.

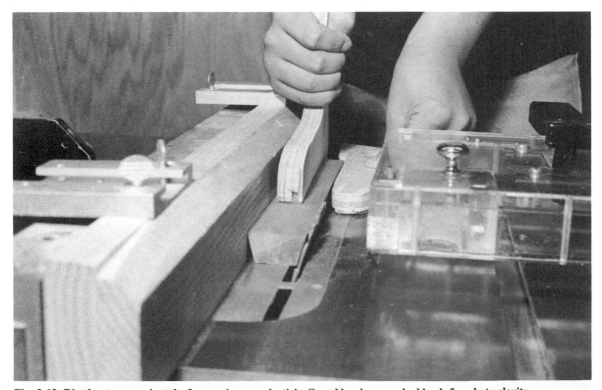

Fig. 2-12. Rip the staves against the fence using a push stick. Guard has been pushed back for photo clarity.

Arrange the staves, side by side, for the best grain patterns. Try to blend one stave into the next. Now number the staves in order, one to twelve, to prevent them from becoming mixed up (Fig. 2-13).

Tape the staves together on the outside with masking tape, so you can roll the bundle together into a cylinder and test the fit of each piece (Fig. 2-14). With good luck and skill, all the parts will fit without further adjustment. Probably, though, tiny errors will compound so that a few staves will not fit just right. This can be fixed during the gluing operation. Leave two opposite stave joints dry without glue. After the glue has set, the canister may be halved at the dry joint and each half section sanded or jointed so the final joint will fit tightly.

The masking tape helps bind the staves together during the gluing operation. Unroll the staves and turn the stack so that the inside of the canister is up. Glue can be applied to the opened beveled joints (Fig. 2-15). Remember that the two opposing joints will remain dry. Roll and unroll the stack several times to spread the glue and then clamp the cylinder with strap clamps (Fig. 2-16). Bicycle inner tubes or automotive worm clamps work well. All the glued seams must fit tightly. It might be necessary to shim the dry joints slightly to make sure the other bevels fit tightly (Fig. 2-17).

When the glue is set, separate the half cylinders and sand or joint the beveled surface to achieve a perfect glue joint. Glue and clamp the half cylinders (Fig. 2-18).

The cylinder is glued to a temporary plywood disk (Fig. 2-19) so that the outside may be turned and one end trued and rabbeted for the real bottom. Check

Fig. 2-13. Number the staves in order.

53

Fig. 2-14. Tape the staves with masking tape.

Fig. 2-15. Glue the open bevel joints.

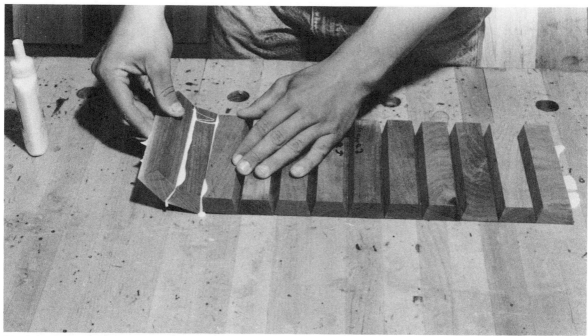

Fig. 2-16. Roll and unroll the stack to spread the glue.

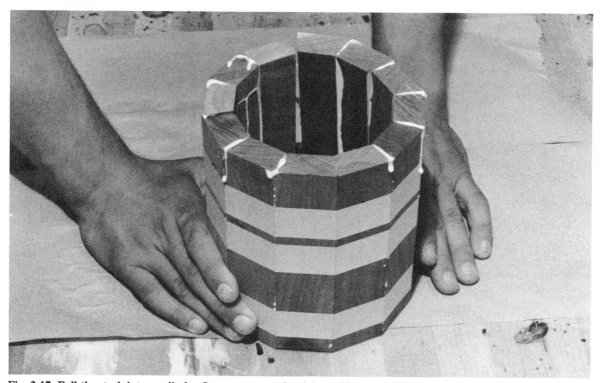

Fig. 2-17. Roll the stack into a cylinder. Leave two opposing joints without glue.

Fig. 2-18. Sand each half cylinder so the final joint is tight.

Fig. 2-19. Glue the cylinder to a plywood disk.

the sides of the cylinder against the plywood disk with a square, and if necessary, sand the end of the cylinder square so that it will not wobble on the lathe. Center a faceplate on the plywood disk and mount the assembly on the lathe. Use another plywood disk, sandwiched between the tailstock and the other end of the cylinder, to stabilize the turning. The second disk need not be glued on; it's there to press the cylinder toward the head stock where only the end grain of the cylinder is glued to the plywood (Fig. 2-20).

Before cutting the cylinder, take time out to prepare blanks for the bottom of the canister and the lid. Cut two circles slightly larger than the diameter of the cylinder out of primary wood. These are each glued to plywood disks with paper in between. The plywood disks are used so that faceplate screws do not penetrate the primary wood; the paper allows easy parting later. The lid has two additional scraps glued to the top that form the knob. Clamp and set these aside so they can be ready when needed (Fig. 2-21).

Go back to the cylinder that is mounted on the lathe. True the outside of the assembly with a gouge (Fig. 2-22). That done, slide the tailstock out of the way and remove the outside disk. This end of the cylinder will become the bottom of the canister. Move the tool rest and true the end of the cylinder with a scraper (Fig. 2-23).

Fig. 2-20. A second plywood disk (unglued) helps stabilize the canister on the lathe.

Fig. 2-21. Glue up the lid and base.

Fig. 2-22. True the outside of the canister with a gouge.

Fig. 2-23. True the end of the canister with a scraper.

Next, move the tool rest to the inside of the cylinder and work inside the canister, at least halfway toward the headstock. What is now the deepest part of the inside, toward the headstock, may be machined later when the plywood disk is parted. A round-nose scraper is handy here. Cut a rabbet $3/8$ inch deep in the tailstock end of the canister to accept the real bottom (Fig. 2-24). Use about half the thickness of the canister wall for the rabbet. Remove the assembly from the lathe.

Fit the bottom blank (that was glued up earlier) to the lathe and turn to fit the rabbet in the canister end. True both the face of the bottom disk and the edge. Cut a rabbet to match the canister bottom end (Fig. 2-25). The canister may be trial fitted to the bottom by sliding the tool rest out of the way, leaving the bottom mounted on the lathe. When the fit is complete, the bottom may be glued to the canister, using the lathe as a clamp. Glue the bottom and canister rabbets and clamp tightly with the tailstock assembly (Fig. 2-26). Leave this to dry for 24 hours.

After the glue is dried, the temporary plywood disk is parted from the tailstock end of the canister. This end of the canister becomes the top (Fig. 2-27). With the disk parted, it is time to cut the inside of the canister—which was hard to reach previously. Smooth the inside (Fig. 2-28).

Fig. 2-24. Cut a rabbet ³/₈ inch deep in the end of the canister.

Fig. 2-25. Mount and cut the bottom to fit the rabbet in canister.

Fig. 2-26. The canister is glued to the bottom.

Fig. 2-27. Part the plywood disk; this end becomes the top.

Fig. 2-28. Scrape and sand the inside of the canister.

Now, direct your attention to the outside of the canister once again. Turn the outside into the curves of the final shape. Finally, cut a rabbet to house the canister lid (Fig. 2-29). Sand inside and out, being careful to keep the lid rabbet edge crisp. Remove the assembly from the lathe.

The lid is turned last (Fig. 2-30). If the faceplate and the plywood disk of the lid stock is smaller than the canister inside diameter, this assembly may be dismounted from the lathe and trial fitted on the canister body to check dimensions. Figure 2-31 shows final fitting of the lid. After the lid is cut and sanded, it is parted from the faceplate. The inside bottom of the lid is sanded on the belt sander. The canister is now ready for finishing (Fig. 2-32). Use a finish safe for use with food.

Fig. 2-29. Shape the outside of the canister and cut a rabbet for the lid.

Fig. 2-30. The lid is turned to fit the rabbet in canister.

Fig. 2-31. Final fitting of the lid.

Fig. 2-32. Ready for sanding and finish.

Fig. 2-33. Wooden bucket.

Project 7: Wooden Bucket

This wooden bucket is made with 18 tapered and beveled staves (Fig. 2-33). All staves are cut in the table saw with two homebuilt jigs. The bottom was cut on the band saw using a circle jig.

Start the bucket by ripping 18 rectangular stave blanks on the table saw. Cut each stave to the size listed. Cut two staves longer than the rest; these will be drilled for the rope handles later (Table 2-5).

Next, cut dados in the bottom inside of each stave for the bottom of the bucket. These are cut before the staves are beveled and tapered. Install a $5/8$-inch dado blade on the table saw arbor and tilt the saw 10 degrees. Using a miter gauge against the fence, cut all the dados (Figs. 2-34 and 2-35).

The jigs illustrated in Figs. 2-36 and 2-37 will hold the staves while the beveled tapers are cut. They are quick to assemble using particle board (or plywood) and drywall screws. One jig does the first beveled taper and the second finishes the opposite beveled taper. Each jig has a base, a tapered stave holder, a handle, and a lever clamp. The base provides a large surface area to slide over the throat plate, a straight edge for contact with the table saw fence, and a surface on which to clamp the stave. The second layer of the jig holds the stave at the correct tapered angle and stops the stave from sliding back. The handle is mounted on top and a lever screwed to the side of the handle. The lever, pivoted at the base of the handle, clamps the stave securely in place during the cut. With the jig, clamping and cutting is a safe one-handed operation. *Note*: The guard has been removed

Table 2-5. Materials List: Wooden Bucket.

NO.	NAME	SIZE	REQ'D
1	STAVE (SHORT)	5/8 X 2 3/16 - 8 5/8 LG	16
2	STAVE (LONG)	5/8 X 2 1/4 - 10 3/4 LG.	2
3	BOTTOM	5/8 X 8 1/2 DIA.	1
4	BINDING (OPTIONAL)	1/8 X 1" - 38 LONG	2
5	TACKS	1/2 LONG	36
6	ROPE-HEMP	3/8 DIA. X 28 LONG	1

STAVE DETAILS
1° MITER
18° SAW BLADE TILT

for photo clarity (Fig. 2-38). A small piece of sandpaper is glued to the base underneath the stave so it does not move during the cut.

After the staves are cut, check the beveled angles. Arrange the staves with the outside up and touching one another on the bench. The row will form an arc (Fig. 2-39). Shift the staves around for the best grain patterns. Make sure the handle staves are nine staves apart so that they will be opposite one another in the finished bucket. Number the staves so they may be reassembled in the same order.

Drill rope holes in the long staves and round the ends as shown. Then tape the outside of the wooden bucket so that the assembly can be rolled up to check the fit of the staves and double check the size of the bottom. With luck the staves will form tight joints with no adjustment, although a slight misalignment will probably show in two staves. This is caused by a tiny error compounded in all the beveled joints. If the gap is small, the bucket may be glued up, leaving two opposite joints dry, without glue.

After the glue has set the halves can be parted and sanded flat for a better fit. Finally, glue the last two joints. Don't forget to taper and fit the bottom of the bucket during the dry assembly stage. The bottom should float in the grove slightly to allow for expansion.

When satisfied with the dry fit, you can glue the bucket. This step is best attempted with the tape on the outside to fold the staves together. Place the stave roll on the bench so the inside is up and the bevel joints are open. Glue the open joints and, if necessary, leave two opposite joints dry to correct any compound errors later. Now roll the staves up around the bottom to form the bucket (Fig. 2-40).

Bicycle inner tubes are fine clamps (Fig. 2-41). Strap clamps, twisted rope or fabric also work well. Check that all the joints are aligned and closed. Shim

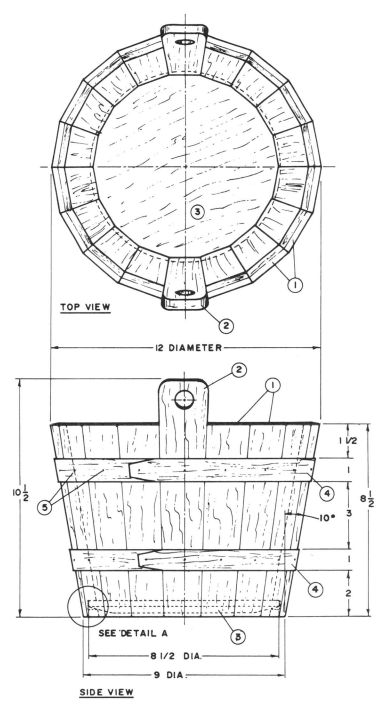

TOP VIEW

12 DIAMETER

SIDE VIEW

SEE DETAIL A

8 1/2 DIA.

9 DIA.

10 1/2

1 1/2

1

3

1

2

8 1/2

10°

Fig. 2-34. Plans for wooden bucket: Top and side views.

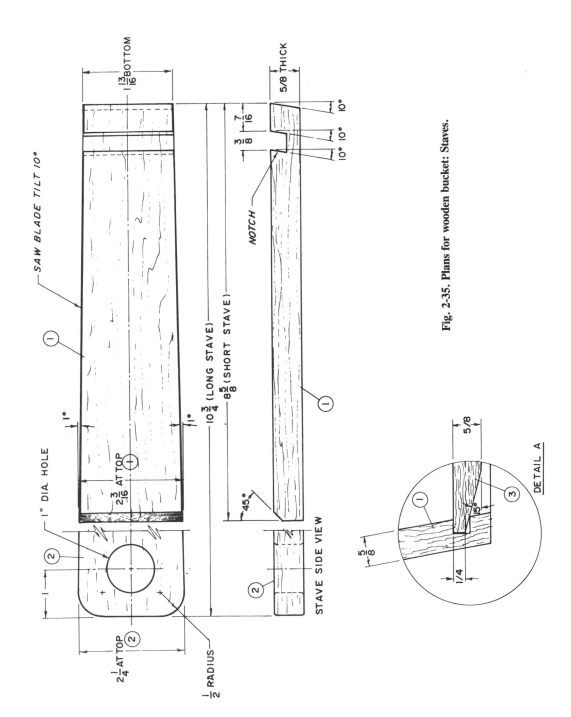

Fig. 2-35. Plans for wooden bucket: Staves.

68

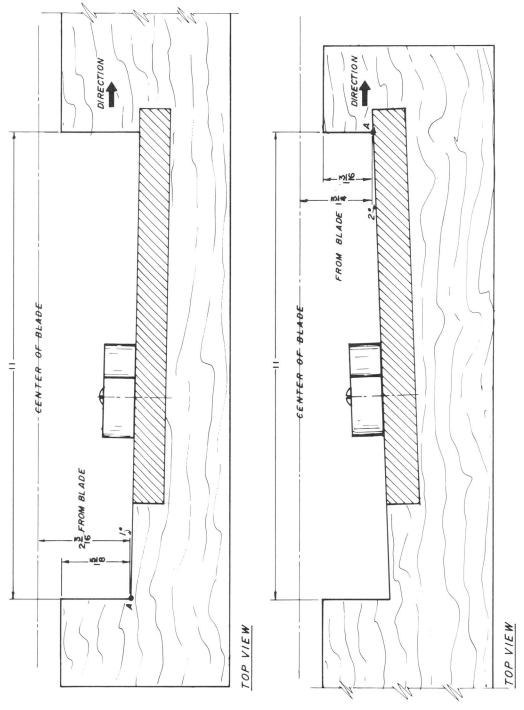

TOP VIEW

TOP VIEW

Fig. 2-36. Jig for cutting beveled taper.

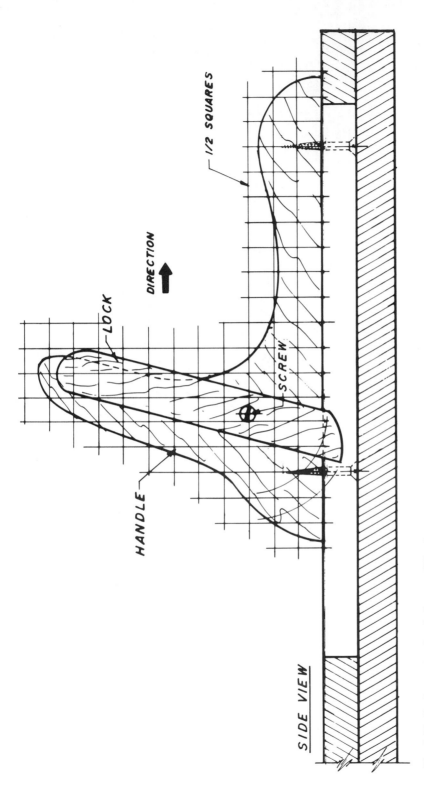

Fig. 2-37. Jig for cutting beveled taper: Side view.

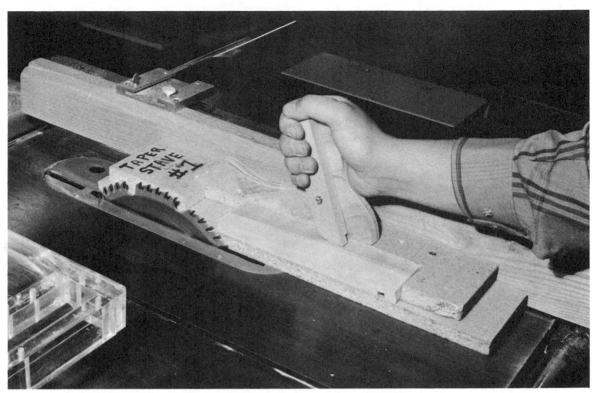

Fig. 2-38. Ripping the staves with a taper jig. Guard has been moved for photo clarity.

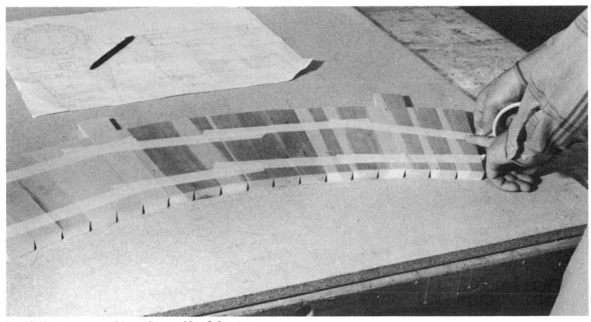

Fig. 2-39. Arrange and tape the outside of the staves.

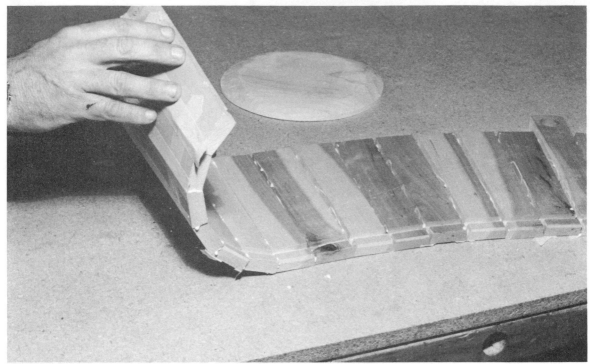

Fig. 2-40. Glue and roll the staves around the bottom.

Fig. 2-41. Bicycle inner tubes make fine clamps.

Fig. 2-42. Plane the outside of the bucket round.

the dry joints, if necessary, to keep all the glue joints together. When the glue is dry, plane the outside of the bucket round (Fig. 2-42).

Hoops on the bucket are optional. Old buckets always had hoops to hold the staves together. Water, milk, or sap swelled the wood tightly against the hoop and the hoop bound the staves tightly together. The staves were not glued and the bucket would not have been a bucket without them!

Project 8: Candy Dish

This candy dish is an evening project (Fig. 2-43). It is an excellent project to practice compound miters on the table saw. The candy dish has four sides and a bottom, supported by the base and pedestal. The base and pedestal are turned on the wood lathe. If the lathe is not available, the base and pedestal may be modified to be square or octagonal, and thus cut on the table saw. Profiles can then be routed in the edges. Close-grained woods, favorable to wood turning, are best for this project.

Start by cutting the parts to size, as listed in the bill of materials (Table 2-6). The sides have bevels on the bottom edge, compound angles in the ends, and curves cut in the top. Cut the compound angles first.

Fig. 2-43. Candy dish.

Table 2-6. Materials List: Candy Dish.

NO.	NAME	SIZE	REQ'D.
I	BASE	3/4 X 5 - 5 LONG	I
2	PEDESTAL	I 3/4 X I 3/4 - 4 I/4 LG.	I
3	SHELF	I/4 X 5 5/8 - 5 5/8 LG.	I
4	SIDES	I/4 X 2 5/8 - 8 I/4 LG.	4
5	SCREW-FLAT HEAD	NO. 8 - I I/4 LONG	2

40° ANGLE OF SIDES   *SEE TABLE 2-1*
    SAW BLADE TILT = 35°
    MITER = 29°

The candy dish has four sides that are sloped at 40 degrees. Locate the four sides on the left of the table and follow to the right until the saw tilt and the miter setting may be read under 40-degree slope. The miter set is 29 degrees and the saw arbor should be tilted to 35 degrees.

74

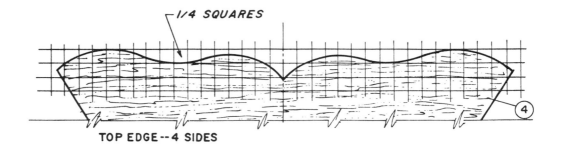

1/4 SQUARES

TOP EDGE -- 4 SIDES

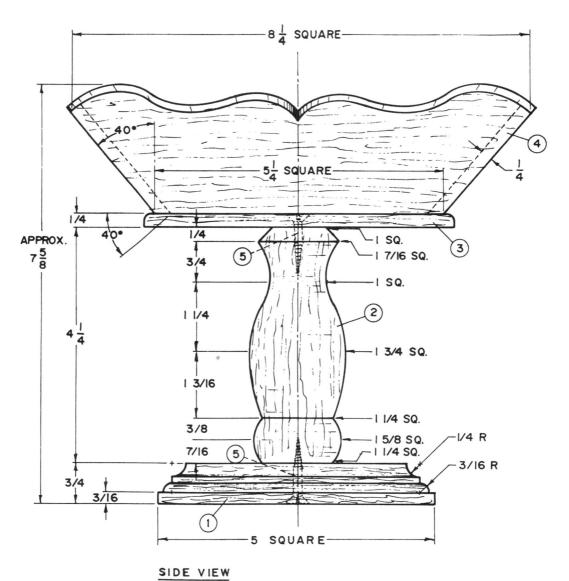

8 1/4 SQUARE

40°

5 1/4 SQUARE

1/4

4

1/4

APPROX.
7 5/8

40°

1/4

1 SQ.

1 7/16 SQ.

5

3/4

1 SQ.

2

1 1/4

1 3/4 SQ.

1 3/16

4 1/4

1 1/4 SQ.

3/8

1 5/8 SQ.

1/4 R

7/16

5

1 1/4 SQ.

3/16 R

3/4

3

1

3/16

5 SQUARE

SIDE VIEW

Fig. 2-44. Plans for candy dish.

75

Screw a hardwood board to the miter gauge so that the side is fully supported during the cut. The board should be long enough to support the cut as the miter gauge is moved from the left of the blade to the right. Clamp the stock to the miter gauge board for the best accuracy for the first cut in each side. During the second cut, use a stop block on the miter gauge board to make sure all the sides are the same length. Try the system first with scrap wood, and check the compound miters in each corner. Adjust if necessary for the final cuts.

Now rip the bottom bevel in the short edge of each side. Tilt the arbor of the saw to 40 degrees and rip a bevel on the outside of each short side. Be sure to use a push stick to guide the stock along the rip fence during the cut.

Lay out the pattern in the top edge of one side. Stack the other three sides underneath the pattern and cut them together. Use masking tape to secure the stack during the cut. Cut the pattern on the band saw or scroll saw. If these machines are not available, a coping saw or saber saw will do the job. File and sand the curves before removing the tape.

Trial fit the sides before gluing. A combination of rubber bands and masking tape will hold the sides together as the glue sets.

While the assembly dries, turn the pedestal and base on the wood lathe—or as mentioned earlier, substitute the turning for a pedestal and base cut on the table saw. Then cut the bottom of the candy dish and round the edges.

Trial fit the bottom to the side assembly. Sand or plane the side edges if there are gaps, then glue the sides to the bottom. Screw the bottom to the pedestal from the inside and counterset the screw flush with the bottom of the dish. The screw holding the base to pedestal can be set in the same way.

Sand and finish the candy dish. Use a food safe nontoxic finish for this project.

3
Cove Cuts

COVES ARE CUT ON THE TABLE SAW BY PASSING STOCK PAST THE TABLE saw blade at an angle. To take a quick check of the possibilities, elevate the table saw blade (disconnect power) and view the blade at table saw height. View the blade left or right up to 90 degrees from the front of the blade. Try this at different blade heights. Any of the profiles you see can be cut out of a piece of wood, if the wood is wide enough so that each shoulder rides on the table surface. The coves may be later ripped or routed to make still other molding profiles.

Figure 3-1 illustrates the setup for the cove cut that is drawn in the end grain of the stock in the background. Fences are clamped on both sides of the stock to guide the cut. It is a good idea to mark the blade area on both fences so that during the cuts hands are never above the blade (Fig. 3-2). Notice a push stick is used to keep the stock to the table. A feather board, pictured in the background, could be used to apply downward pressure as well.

When the setup is finished, crank the top of the blade to table level for the first cut. Cut the cove in repeated passes, raising the blade slightly between cuts (Fig. 3-3). The idea is to cut a little with each pass, without straining the saw or the table saw motor. Make the last cuts with slow feed speeds to produce the best finish possible. Smooth the cove with a convex scraper blade; finish with sandpaper.

Fig. 3-1. Table saw setup for a cove cut.

Fig. 3-2. Never pass hands above the blade.

Fig. 3-3. Repeat passes, raising blade slightly between each pass.

Project 9: Pennsylvania Dutch Hope Chest

Note: This is the most complicated project in the book. Construction time is twice as long as you expect. Like other projects, however, it is constructed one step at a time and no step is too difficult. It is a delightful project that will last for generations (Fig. 3-4).

As my daughter approached 16, I felt it was time to follow in the footsteps of past generations and make her a hope chest. I turned to my friend, John Nelson, to design a chest practical for a small home. The design of this chest was inspired by one built by John Bachman of Lancaster County, Pennsylvania. His blanket chest was of walnut with a sulphur inlay in the front, indicating the chest was probably made for his daughter in 1784. The original chest was 4 feet long. Working from photographs of the chest, John scaled the chest to 32 inches wide, 14 inches deep, and 20 inches high, a size suitable for a smaller room or bedroom. He was not able to get information about the inside of the chest, and therefore designed a hinged box inside the chest typical of others made at the time. The corner dovetail layout, drawer size, and moldings copy the original chest by

Fig. 3-4. Pennsylvania Dutch hope chest.

Bachman. The scaled bracketed feet appeared too large, and a bit out of proportion. I was tempted to make them smaller, but in the end decided to keep to scale.

Native American woods should be used for this Early American project. Walnut is the best choice, if it is affordable and available. Bachman's original chest was of walnut. Lacking walnut, I chose a cherry wood. Other choices are tiger or bird's-eye maple, or chestnut. Birch or poplar could be used for the primary wood. The secondary woods—used for the drawer sides and bottom, as well as the bottom panels of the chest—should be clear pine or poplar. The secondary wood is chosen for lightness and workability, as well as to keep the cost of the primary wood down.

Once the primary wood is chosen, lay the stock around the shop and spend time choosing all parts of the chest (Figs. 3-5 and 3-6). Flip boards, examine the back, and check color and grain patterns. Try to lay out the front and sides from the same board so that the grain will follow around corners. Match drawer fronts with the front board, and with themselves so that the grain flows from one drawer front to the next. Select straight-grain stock for molding parts, so they will be easy to machine. Some waste is inevitable; accept it. Keep the finished chest in mind and lay out for pleasing grain orientation, patterns, and color.

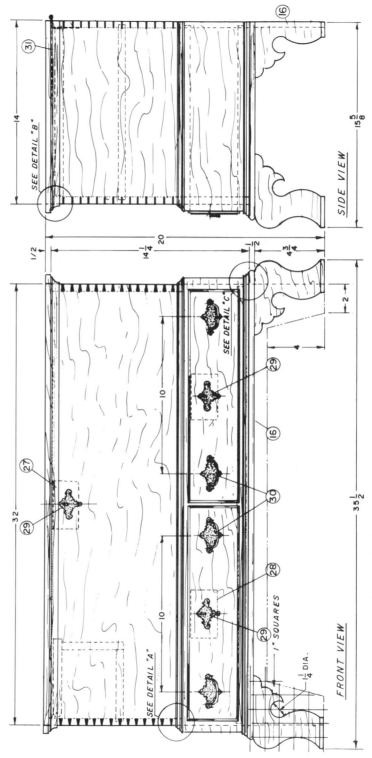

Fig. 3-5. Plans for hope chest: Front and side views.

81

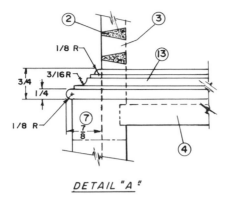

DETAIL "A"

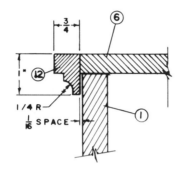

DETAIL "B"

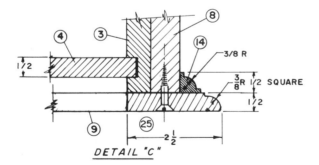

DETAIL "C"

Fig. 3-6. Plans for hope chest: Details.

Make economy of parts a second priority. The back board and the back surface of parts that glue to the chest need not be perfect. The dovetails should be cut in strong, defect-free parts. The time spent in this first stage can make the difference between an ordinary piece and a spectacular one.

During this process, mark each part in pencil so they can be easily found later. Hope for the best. Remember mistakes do happen and alternatives must be chosen.

In a reproduction chest, the final wood surface should not show modern tool marks, such as scalloping from planers or jointers. Circular marks from the table saw, chatter marks from the router, or swirl marks from sanding are equally distracting. In 1784, wood surfaces were smoothed with hand planes or scrapers. In the larger shops, the work was done by apprentices and the parts turned over to the master for jointwork and assembly. Thank goodness for our modern powered surfacing machines! After the boards are machined and surfaced, plane the surface with a slightly convex hand plane before the parts are ripped, and crosscut to finished size.

Hand planing surfaces is simply enjoyable. This step will save much finishing time after the chest is assembled, and will better acquaint you with the characteristics of the wood before the joint work is done.

Lay the parts out on a clean, smooth surface at a good workable height (Table 3-1). Use a hand plane with a slightly convex blade to smooth surfaces and remove machine marks. The convex blade, used with scrub planes, leaves a lightly scalloped surface with smooth edges. I use a Stanley smooth plane with the iron ground slightly convex. If the plane is adjusted well and the iron is sharp, the results will be better than with sanding machines, and not take any longer.

Work across the surface, overlapping strokes. Then check the board across a light source to see if all machine marks are removed. Some woods will have trouble with grain tear, especially around knots. Try approaching these areas from the opposite direction, even changing direction over a knot, with a freshly honed plane iron. If grain tear is persistent in a small area, try belt sanding the grain tear out, then dressing the surface with a freshly prepared scraper blade.

Once the stock is chosen and planed, work toward subassembly (Figs. 3-7 and 3-8). All other parts are cut to fit the basic box shape later. Cut parts 1, 2, 3 first, and square and size accurately. Then lay out and cut the corner dovetails.

Dovetail details are laid out in the plans. Scribe the dovetail out with a sharp knife. Although there are several good ways to cut dovetails, I chose to cut the tails (parts 1 and 2) first and scribe the pins from the tails (part 3). Laying out and cutting the 74 dovetails will be the most time-consuming task of the chest construction. I found it easiest to make a brass and wood gauge, so that the tails would be as close as possible to the original layout. Clearly mark each waste area so there is no mistaking which side of the line to cut. Scribe the depth of each tail and pin (inside and out) slightly deeper than the board thickness. They will stand above the finished joint and can be planed smooth to the surface later.

Mark each corner of the chest by number (on the outside) to its mate, so that each time a board is handled it is clear what corner it is, and where the outside surface is.

Cut each dovetail down to the scribe line and remove the waste. I used a dovetail saw, cutting on the waste side of each line. The part being cut was securely clamped between two hardwood blocks, each jointed and fitted at the scribe line. That way I would not cut too deep, and the depth of each dovetail was the same.

Remove the waste between the dovetails next. I used the band saw to nibble

Table 3-1. Materials List: Hope Chest.

NO.	NAME	SIZE	REQ'D.
1	FRONT	5/8 X 9 5/8 - 32 LG.	1
2	BACK	5/8 X 14 1/4 - 32 LG.	1
3	SIDE	5/8 X 14 1/4 - 14 LG.	2
4	DIVIDER - HORIZONTAL	1/2 X 13 1/2 - 31 1/4 LG.	2
5	DIVIDER - VERTICAL	1/2 X 3 3/4 - 13 1/8 LG.	2
6	LID	5/8 X 14 1/16 - 32 1/8	1
7	SKIRT - FRONT	3/4 X 4 3/4 - 33 1/2	1
8	SKIRT - SIDE	3/4 X 4 3/4 - 14 3/4	2
9	BASE - FRONT	1/2 X 2 1/2 - 35 3/4	1
10	BASE - SIDE	1/2 X 2 1/2 - 15 7/8	2
11	BASE - REAR	1/2 X 2 1/2 - 31 3/4	1
12	MOLDING - LID	3/4 X 1 - 72 LONG	1
13	MOLDING WAIST	3/4 X 7/8 - 72 LG.	1
14	MOLDING BOTTOM	1/2 X 1/2 - 72 LONG	1
15	FOOT BRACE	1 1/2 X 4 3/4 - 36 LG.	1
16	BACK SUPPORT	3/4 X 4 3/4 - 34 1/4	1
17	BLOCK	3/4 X 1 1/4 - 1 1/4 LG.	12
18	BOTTOM	1/2 X 5 - 13 1/4 LG	1
19	FACE	1/2 X 4 1/2 - 13 1/4	1
20	LID	1/2 X 5 5/8 - 12 3/4	1
21	DRAWER - SIDE	1/2 X 3 3/16 - 13 1/4	2
22	DRAWER - BACK	1/2 X 3 3/16 - 14 9/16	1
23	DRAWER - BOTTOM	3/8 X 12 1/2 - 13 3/4	1
24	DRAWER - FRONT	3/4 X 3 7/16 - 15 9/16	1
25	SCREW - FLAT HD.	NO. 8 - 1 1/4 LONG	AS REQ'D.
26	FINISH NAIL	6 d	2
27	CHEST LOCK	STYLE "J" TJB-063	1
28	DRAWER LOCK	STYLE "F" TFB-028	2
29	ESCUTCHEON	STYLE "S" S23-043	3
30	DRAWER PULL	STYLE "S" S23-043	4
31	HINGE 9" SIZE	H 37 - C 50	1 PR.
32	HINGE PIN	3/16 DIA. X 3/4 LG.	1

PURCHASE PART NOS. 27, 28, 29, 30 AND 31 FROM:
BALL AND BALL
463 W. LINCOLN HIGHWAY
EXTON, PENNSYLVANA 19341

TEL. (215) - 363-7330

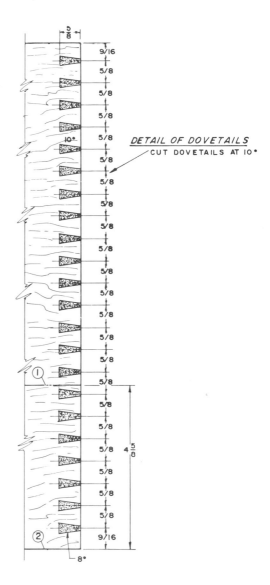

Fig. 3-7. Plans for hope chest: Subassembly.

DETAIL OF DOVETAILS
CUT DOVETAILS AT 10°

out most of the waste and finished up with a sharp chisel. This technique works later with the pins if the band saw table is tilted or jigged both ways.

When the dovetails are cut and cleaned, the pins may be marked. Clamp the dovetail over the pin board and scribe the pins from the dovetails. Here it is important that the clamping be rigid and flat. I clamped the end grain of the pin board flush with a hardwood block on the inside, then clamped the dovetail board flat down on top of this. With a sharp knife, scribe the pins in their end grain. Release the clamps and scribe the pins with a square to the depth line previously scribed. Do this on both sides of the board. Mark the waste in pencil.

Use the dovetail saw to cut down on the waste side of each pin. Again, clamp two hardwood blocks on each side of the board, at the scribe line, to avoid cutting

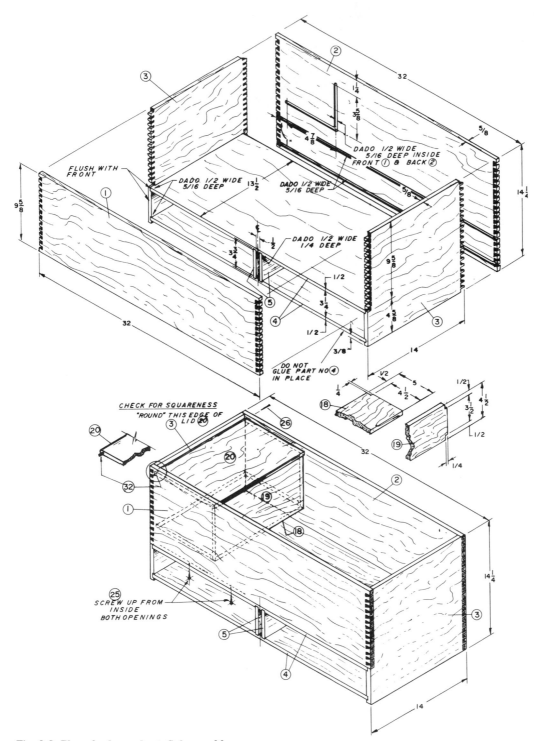

Fig. 3-8. Plans for hope chest: Subassembly.

too deep. The waste between the pins may be cut away on the band saw with the table tilted to 10 degrees. Some band saws do not tilt both ways, however. A tapered board (10 degrees) underneath the pin board will do the trick. The last of the waste is cleaned up with a narrow chisel. During the final chiseling operation, it is helpful to reclamp the two hardwood blocks next to the scribe line. These blocks not only guide the chisel, but also avoid damaging the back side of the pin board.

Trial fit each mated dovetail corner and trim any pins that are too tight. If a dovetail is too loose, try gluing a small chip to the side of the dovetail and trimming with a chisel later (Fig. 3-9).

Next, the dados must be cut to house the chest bottoms (part 4) and interior box (parts 18 and 19). The dados (plows) are stopped at the ends to avoid the dovetails. Parts 4, 18, and 19 are notched at their corners to fit the stopped dados. The double router track keeps the router from wandering.

The bottoms (part 4) should be cut so there is room for seasonal cross grain movement in the dado at the back of the chest. If the wood is dry and the season is dry, make provisions for expansion. Therefore, the bottom (part 4) should not fit all the way to the bottom of the dado groove in the chest back; it should just enter the dado and stop. It will be flush with the front. Conversely, if construction is in humid times, the bottom should fill the dado in the back board so that it can shrink later. The outside of the hope chest, length and depth, will remain stable because the grain of the front, back, and sides runs around the chest.

The dividers (part 5) are dadoed using the same router and double fence technique. Although the plans do not show this, here is an opportunity to develop a hidden compartment. If the dados in part 4 were *not* cut, part 5 could be made into a narrow hidden box that might slide out of the drawer opening (sideways) after both drawers were removed. The drawers may also be constructed with hidden compartments, and will be discussed later.

Dry fit the subassembly (Figs. 3-7 and 3-8) of the chest sides, bottoms, and interior compartment. When satisfied, cut scrap boards to clamp the corner dovetails together. Clamp the chest together without glue to test the clamping arrangement. Evenly distributed pressure should close all the dovetail joints. When the clamping system is satisfactory, the chest may be pulled apart, glued, and reclamped. This, especially with quick setting yellow glue, is a two-person job.

Once clamped up, check the case for squareness. Correct if necessary by shifting clamps. When the case is dry, plane down the end grain of the dovetails (those that stand above the surface) with a block plane.

Now refer to Fig. 3-9. Cut and apply the skirt (parts 7 and 8). Miter the corners. The miters may be splined to increase strength or, as in Fig. 3-10, the miters can be strengthened with a sliding dovetail. This will be hidden by the molding (part 13). The original chest probably had plain miters in the skirt corner.

A router table and an assortment of bits is necessary to make molding. It might be efficient to cut all moldings at one time. Cut the skirt waist (part 13), skirt bottom (part 14), base side (part 10), and the lid (part 12). Note, however,

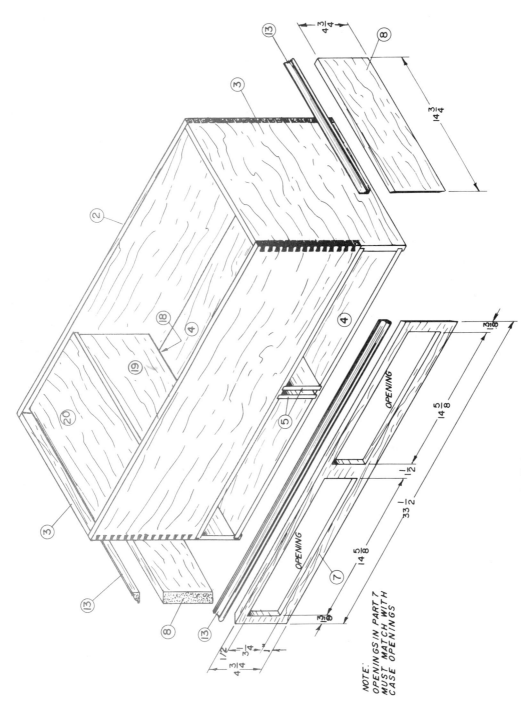

NOTE:
OPENINGS IN PART 7
MUST MATCH WITH
CASE OPENINGS

Fig. 3-9. Plans for hope chest: Pieces ready for fitting.

Fig. 3-10. The base miters have been strengthened with optional sliding dovetails.

the molding around the lid is not mitered, but is butted at the front corner (Fig. 3-11). Thus, the molding strips are glued to the top before they are routed.

Fastening the molding strips around the top board (part 6) needs further explanation. The front strip that runs with the grain of the top will be no problem, but the strips on the ends of the top board cross the grain of the top need extra attention. Because the top will expand and contract over the seasons, these end strips can work loose, or pop the corner joint. One way to avoid problems is to apply glue to only the first 6 inches of the side strip from the front corner. Nail the rear section. The finish nails will have enough give to allow the top to expand and contract. Remember: Nail where the router bit won't strike metal when cutting the molding.

Glue and nail on the base skirts (parts 7 and 8), and waist molding (part 13). The assembly is complete.

The base of the chest is made up and screwed to the main body from underneath. Start with the chest feet, which are cut from the cove molding shown in the profile (part 15). This cove molding is cut on the table saw. First cut the cove in the foot brace board. Then cut the front four miters on the table saw with the blade tilted to 45 degrees and the part guided with the miter gauge. Set the blade back to 90 degrees, crosscut the back legs and cut the rabbets. Finally lay out and

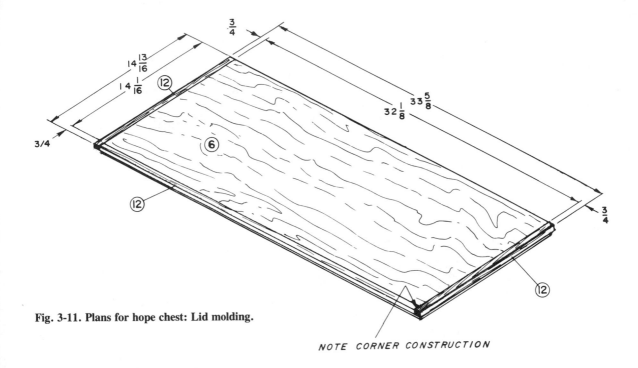

Fig. 3-11. Plans for hope chest: Lid molding.

NOTE CORNER CONSTRUCTION

cut the curved design. Drill a 1¼-inch hole in each leg and finish the design on the band saw.

Glue the front miters and reinforce with a stack of small blocks, each with grain running parallel to the grain in the foot (Fig. 3-12). Glue the rear legs and nail to part 16. Fasten the base boards (parts 10 and 11) with splined miters (Fig. 3-13) in the front and an open mortise-and-tenon in the rear. The spline slots may be cut on the horizontal router arrangement, and the rear mortise-and-tenon joints cut with the same techiques used for the panel door construction (Fig. 3-14).

When the base is finished, the feet are glued and screwed up from beneath, and the assembly attached to the chest with screws from below (Figs. 3-15 and 3-16). Then the last of the molding (part 14) is cut, nailed, and glued in place.

Drawers are sized to fit the dimensions cut in the front skirt (part 7). Recheck the opening before the drawers are constructed. Figure 3-17 shows one drawer construction method, with dovetail construction (half blind in the front and through in the back), and the bottom housed on four sides with room for drawer expansion and contraction across the grain.

As previously mentioned, we worked from photos of the complete original, and can only guess as to the construction of the drawer interiors. Therefore, we will explore several alternatives.

The drawer bottom should be thicker in the middle and feathered in the sides to be housed in the dado groove. The grain runs across the drawer. It was common in drawer construction to cut the back of the drawer short in width so that

Fig. 3-12. Small blocks reinforce feet.

Fig. 3-13. Baseboards are joined with splined miters.

Fig. 3-14. Open mortise-and-tenon joints in the rear of the baseboards.

Fig. 3-15. Baseboards are screwed to the feet.

the bottom ran underneath the drawer back and was nailed up from underneath. The back of the drawer had no dado (or plough) groove (Fig. 3-18).

To make the chest intriguing for my daughter, I added hidden compartments to the drawer. Near the end of each drawer I dadoed in a false drawer back. If the

Fig. 3-16. The subassembly is screwed to the chest.

drawer is prevented from coming out of the chest, the false drawer back appears to be the back of the drawer. This arrangement was achieved by drilling a hole in the underside of the hope chest so that a spring-loaded dowel would stop the drawer from coming out too far. The bottom of the drawer is stopped grooved, to house the dowel that springs up from the bottom of the chest. The drawer is released by sliding one hand beneath the chest, and pulling the dowel down. The drawer can then be removed and the hidden compartment exposed.

Another way to make a hidden drawer is to construct a false bottom. Machine two dado grooves in the sides of the drawer. Cut the back of the drawer short in width with the top dado machined. When the drawer is constructed with two bottoms, the lower one can slide out below the back, revealing a shallow hidden compartment. Needless to say, this works best with deep drawers. This isn't the best alternative for the hope chest, because the drawer is too shallow. Whatever method you use, be sure to cut the mortise for the lock before the drawer is glued up.

Hardware can now be installed in the drawers and the chest lid. Recesses are mortised out for the chest and drawer locks, as well as the lid hinges. Use patience and good craftsmanship here. Hardware must fit correctly for good locking and smooth hinge swing. Install the locks first, and use graphite on the

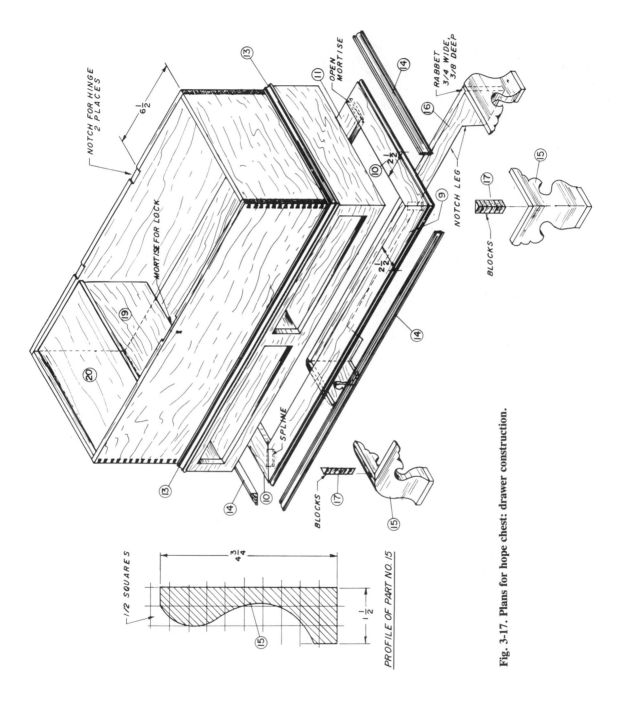

NOTCH FOR HINGE 2 PLACES

6½

MORTISE FOR LOCK

13

11

OPEN MORTISE

13

14

RABBET 3/4 WIDE, 3/8 DEEP

16

2½

10

NOTCH LEG

9

15

17

BLOCKS

19

20

SPLINE

13

14

10

14

17

BLOCKS

15

15

17

BLOCKS

1/2 SQUARES

4¾

1½

15

PROFILE OF PART NO. 15

Fig. 3-17. Plans for hope chest: drawer construction.

94

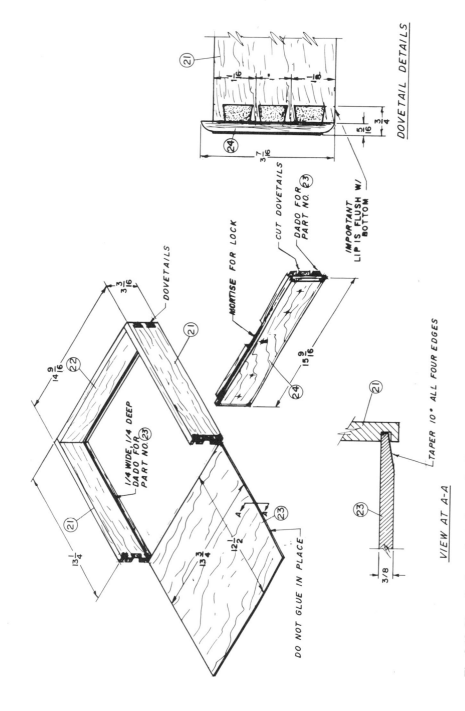

DOVETAIL DETAILS

DO NOT GLUE IN PLACE

DOVETAILS

3/16

14 9/16

1/4 WIDE, 1/4 DEEP
DADO FOR
PART NO. 23

13 1/4

13 3/4

12 1/2

MORTISE FOR LOCK

CUT DOVETAILS

DADO FOR
PART NO. 23

IMPORTANT
LIP IS FLUSH W/
BOTTOM

15 9/16

3 7/16

3/4

5/16

1/16   1/16

TAPER 10° ALL FOUR EDGES

3/8

VIEW AT A-A

Fig. 3-18. Plans for hope chest: drawer detail.

95

lock pins to locate position for the strike plates. The strike plates are also mortised in.

The chest is ready for finishing. Always experiment on scrap wood first. Stain may be chosen to change color. Urethane is a durable finish, when applied in multiple thin coats. I chose to finish with Watco clear oil finish. The oil is easy to apply and the surface hardens in time. Finally, wax the surface. And if you like, sign your name in an inconspicuous place.

4

The Jerry Joint

THE JERRY JOINT, USED IN THE LID OF THE ROUND-TOP CHEST, IS AN EASY WAY to provide a dust lip for boxes and chests. The jerry joint secures the lid in small boxes without requiring hardware.

The jerry joint is cut in two stages. First, a plow or dado is cut inside the box before the box is assembled. The box is assembled with the lid glued in place. Then after assembly, the box is cut open with the second dado cut, freeing the lid assembly, complete with dust lip. This process is described fully in the techniques for the round-top chest.

Project 10: Round-Top Chest

The round-top chest featured here is made in eastern white pine, and painted with early New England colors and designs (Fig. 4-1). The overall design of this chest is similar to those made 200 years ago. The major variation is the unique dust stop lip used between the chest and the lid. This dust stop, which we call a *jerry joint*, is cut into the chest during construction of the parts. In years past, a $1/4$-×-1-inch board was nailed around the inside of the chest to create a dust stop.

Many of the country chests of early colonial times were fastened together with butt joints and hand-forged nails. Some of the cruder chests had the bottoms nailed on from below, leaving a visible joint all around the chest! Possibly the survival of the cruder chests was the result of storage in a dusty attic, rather than years of active use. The craftsmen who made chests had varied skills, which is reflected in the diverse construction jointery observed in surviving chests.

Fig. 4-1. Round-top chest.

The chest for this project features the use of butt, rabbet, and dado (often referred as "plow") joints throughout, which make a strong, well-constructed chest. Yet the project itself is simple to make. The chest bottom is rabbeted and housed loosely in a plow joint cut inside the chest. Thin strips of oak are nailed to the bottom of the chest to hide the bottom expansion joint and to provide wear resistance (Table 4-1).

A special feature is the rabbeted dust lip separating the lid from the chest. This joint, the jerry joint, is actually started before the chest is assembled, and finished when the lid is sawn from the body of the chest (Fig. 4-2). The jerry joint is cut on the table saw at the same time as the bottom plow groove. The rabbeted corners add a nice sophistication to the chest. The plow groove is a dado that is cut with the grain of the wood. The chest may be constructed in a few evenings (Figs. 4-3 and 4-4).

Stronger corner joints, such as the box or dovetail, could be used if the length of the end parts is increased. If dovetail or box joints are chosen, the plow

Table 4-1. Materials List: Round-Top Chest.

NO.	N A·M E	S I Z E	REQ'D
1	END	5/8 X 15 5/8 – 11 3/8 LG.	2
2	FRONT / BACK	5/8 X 14 3/16 – 22 LONG	2
3	BOTTOM	5/8 X 11 1/4 – 21 3/8 LG.	1
4	TOP	3/8 X 1 1/8 – 22 LONG	12
5	FOOT	3/16 X 3/4 – 22 LONG	3

grooves for the bottom and inside dust lip must be stopped so that the groove does not show on the outside of the chest. The chest lid is eventually separated from the body of the chest with a 5/16-inch-wide dado blade cut, so it is important to lay out the dovetails carefully from the beginning. The dovetail joint, which is cut open, should be 5/16-inch wider than the others, because after the final cut the lid will settle down on the chest by the width of the dado cut (Fig. 4-5).

The surface condition of the chest is as important to the finished appearance as the painting. If the chest is to look old, all surfaces must be hand planed after

Fig. 4-2. Jerry joint dust lip.

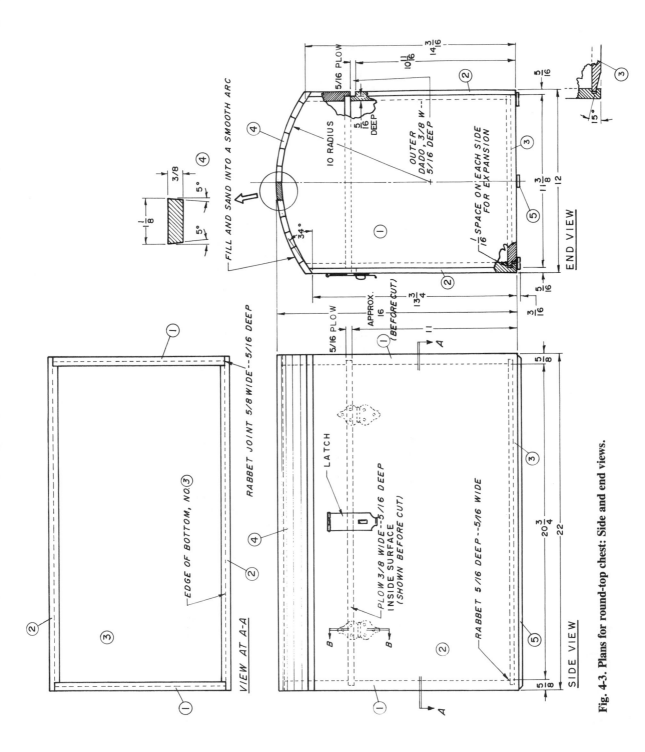

Fig. 4-3. Plans for round-top chest: Side and end views.

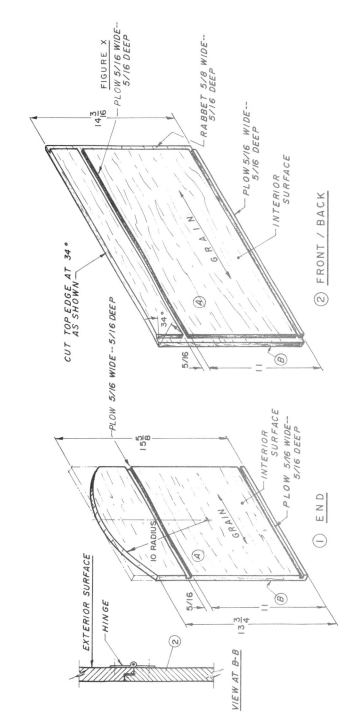

FIGURE X

PLOW 5/16 WIDE--
5/16 DEEP

RABBET 5/8 WIDE--
5/16 DEEP

PLOW 5/16 WIDE--
5/16 DEEP

INTERIOR
SURFACE

14 3/16

GRAIN

Ⓐ

34°

5/16

11

Ⓑ

② FRONT / BACK

CUT TOP EDGE AT 34°
AS SHOWN

PLOW 5/16 WIDE--5/16 DEEP

15 5/8

PLOW 5/16 WIDE--
5/16 DEEP

INTERIOR
SURFACE

GRAIN

10 RADIUS

Ⓐ

5/16

11

Ⓑ

① END

13 3/4

EXTERIOR SURFACE

HINGE

②

VIEW AT B-B

Fig. 4-4. Plans for round-top chest: End and front/back views.

101

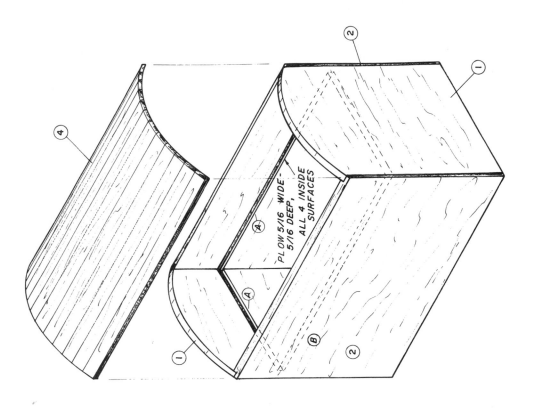

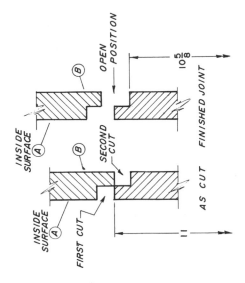

PLOW 5/16 WIDE—
5/16 DEEP,
ALL 4 INSIDE
SURFACES

OPEN
POSITION

$10\frac{5}{8}$

FINISHED JOINT

INSIDE
SURFACE

SECOND
CUT

AS CUT

INSIDE
SURFACE

FIRST CUT

11

Fig. 4-5. Plans for round-top chest.

the wood is machined. Painted surfaces, more than other finishes, telescope irregularities of the wood. Smooth ridges and valleys, planed by hand, authentically copy original work. Smooth, slightly uneven hand-planed surfaces reflect light in warm, eye-pleasing textures. Regular scalloped machine planer marks or a flat sanded surface showing through the paint reveal this as a newly made piece, which is in contrast with the design and the painting style.

I prefer hand planing the parts before assembly. Consider a project from start to finish, without sanding! The hand plane, scraper, and perhaps a piece of broken glass is all that is needed.

If wide stock is not available, start by gluing up stock for the two ends (part 1), front/back (part 2), and the bottom (part 3). If possible, avoid knots; they tend to be a nuisance both in surfacing and painting. It might be easier to glue up the bottom and front/back in one panel, and the ends in a separate panel. If a thickness planer is available, glue up $3/4$-inch stock and plane the panels to slightly greater than $5/8$-inch thickness. Then the panels may be hand surfaced to $5/8$ inch before the parts are cut out.

Hand surfacing is done with a scrub plane. I use a smooth plane with the iron sharpened convex so that its edges do not contact the wood. This leaves a surface with gentle ridges and valleys. Start at one edge of the panel and move across in long, gentle strokes, covering the entire surface. Check the finished panel against reflected light to make sure all machine planer marks are removed.

Cut the parts to rectangular size listed in the bill of materials. Delay cutting the radius in the end parts (1) and edge bevel of the front/back (part 2) until all the other joint work is done.

Next, the joint work is machined, in two settings of the dado head on the table saw. If you don't have a dado head, make repeating cuts using a single blade, merely adjusting the fence between cuts.

To make bottom plow grooves, set the dado head at $5/16$ inch wide and adjust to $5/16$ inch deep. Identify and mark the bottom inside of the ends and front/back parts. Turn cupped boards so that the concave side is toward the inside of the chest. Rip the bottom plow groove in the ends and the front/back parts at the same time, leaving $5/16$ inch of wood between the groove and bottom edge (Fig. 4-6). Keep the bottom of each part toward the fence.

For the inside dust lip, reset the fence (leave the blade at the same setting) and rip the grooves for the dust lip (Fig. 4-7). Again, keep the bottom of the parts toward the fence. This way all grooves will line up during assembly. During this operation it is important that any parts that are cupped be held flat against the table saw surface. During assembly cupped parts will be pulled flat again and the plow grooves will line up. At this time, cut and mark a story stick (Fig. 4-8). When the chest is nailed together the story stick will locate exactly where the lid is to be parted with the dado blade.

For bottom rabbets, reset the fence next to the dado head and cut the rabbets on all four sides of the bottom. An alternative to this, used often in old drawer parts, is to bevel the bottom panel. The panel will be inserted into the groove, thin at the edge and thick in the middle.

Fig. 4-6. Rip the groove for the bottom.

Fig. 4-7. Rip the inside dust lip.

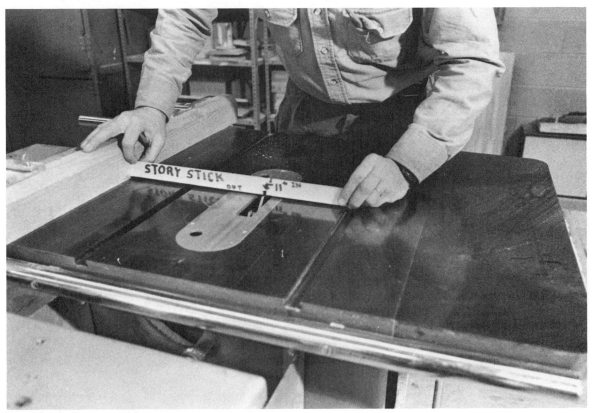

Fig. 4-8. Mark a story stick.

For corner rabbets, set the dado head at $^5/_8$-inch wide and $^5/_{16}$-inch deep. Cut the rabbets across the grain in the front/back to accept the end parts. Figure 4-9 illustrates the plow grooves and corner rabbets cut.

Remove the dado head from the table saw, and rip the 34-degree angle at the top of the front/back parts (Fig. 4-10). Locate and draw the radius in the end parts and cut the rounded top on the band saw.

The top parts may be resawn from $^3/_4$-inch boards or planed down to $^3/_8$-inch thickness. Hand plane the larger boards first, then rip the parts on the table saw with the blade tilted 5 degrees. After the first two cuts, test fit the pieces on the curve of the end piece. Adjust the angle of the blade if necessary and continue cutting all 12 parts.

The chest is ready for assembly (Fig. 4-11). Test fit the ends, front/back, and bottom. The bottom should float free in the bottom groove. If the chest is assembled in low humidity (in our area that's winter), it should float very free, especially across the grain. During the humid summer the bottom will swell across the grain $^1/_4$ inch. Glue the corner joints and nail the chest together around the bottom. Finish nails can be used. Countersink and fill them. Alternatively, use square cut nails, driven and left on the surface. Do not nail in the corners where the lid will be cut off.

Fig. 4-9. Cut the corner rabbets.

Fig. 4-10. Rip the 34-degree angle at the top of the front/back parts.

106

Fig. 4-11. Assemble the sides and bottom.

Fig. 4-12. Mark the point the lid will be cut off.

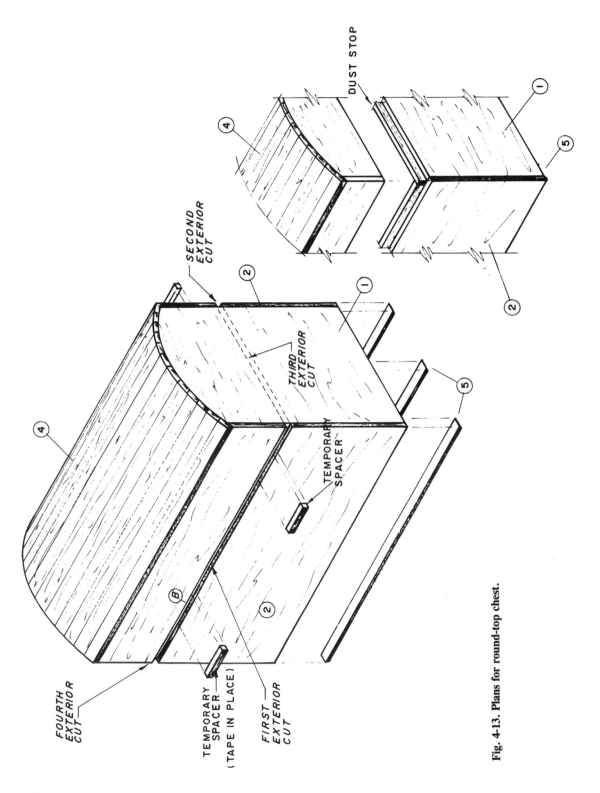

DUST STOP

④

①

⑤

②

SECOND EXTERIOR CUT

②

THIRD EXTERIOR CUT

①

TEMPORARY SPACER

⑤

④

B

②

TEMPORARY SPACER
(TAPE IN PLACE)

FIRST EXTERIOR CUT

FOURTH EXTERIOR CUT

Fig. 4-13. Plans for round-top chest.

Fig. 4-14. Taped blocks space the lid during final cut.

Fig. 4-15. The finished lid.

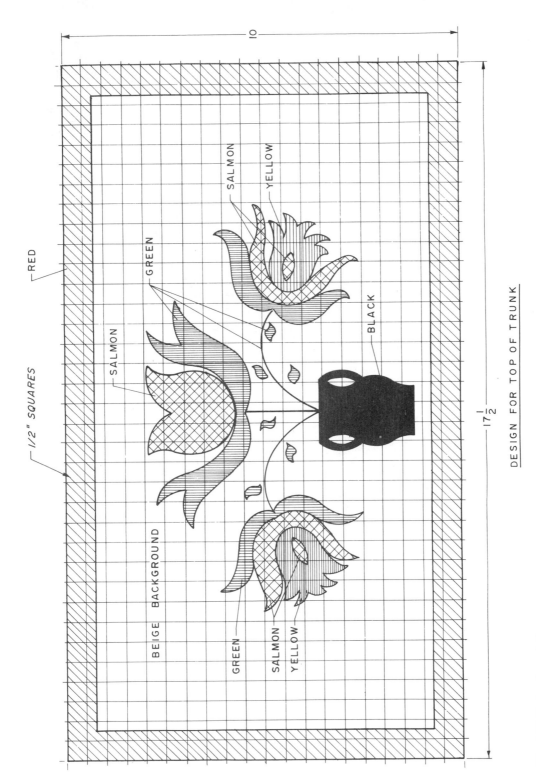

Fig. 4-16. Design for painting.

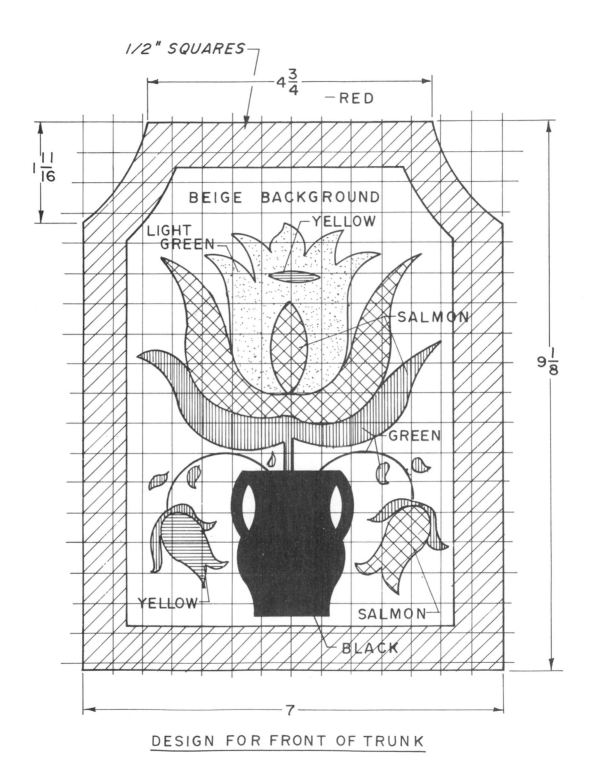

DESIGN FOR FRONT OF TRUNK

Fig. 4-17. Design for painting.

The story stick helps locate the inside plow groove; the chest will be cut open below this plow groove (Fig. 4-12). The bottom should not be glued, but it may be secured with one finish nail into the center of each end, driven when the bottom panel is centered in the groove. The nail will hold the bottom panel on center so that, over the seasons, it will move equally on both front and back grooves.

Next, glue and nail the top slats in place over the curved ends. Start in the top center and work toward the edges. Trim the last pieces to the lid with a hand plane.

Cut the chest open on the table saw, against the fence, using a dado blade. Set the dado blade at $5/6$ inch wide and a shade higher than $5/16$ inch. If the sides of the chest are $5/8$ inch thick, this will leave a little clearance in the dust lip. Check this setup on scrap wood.

You will be cutting below the first plow groove on the inside of the chest. Here the story stick comes in handy. As the chest is cut open, insert and tape a temporary spacer as shown in Fig. 4-13. This will keep the lid and bottom spaced properly during the final cuts. Figure 4-14 illustrates the taped blocks, and in Fig. 4-15 the finished lid is cut off.

After the lid is cut off, it should fit snugly down on the dust seal. Use a rabbeting plane to remove the saw marks and to develop a slight hinge clearance. Nail on the bottom strips and chamfer their ends.

Trim and smooth the outside of the chest for painting. Remember, it is best not to use sandpaper. The appearance of hand tool marks on the surface should show through the paint. This chest was painted by Nancy Van Campen in Early American colors on a black satin background. We have included Nancy's designs and colors for those readers who wish to copy her work (Figs. 4-16 and 4-17).

II

Band Saw Techniques

THE BAND SAW RIVALS THE TABLE SAW AS THE MOST-USED MACHINE IN MY shop. Students who use the shop start by crosscutting, ripping, and contour sawing with the band saw. As they increase their skills and try more difficult projects, they begin to resaw, pattern saw, and set up jigs and fixtures on the band saw for all kinds of special needs. This machine, with a narrow blade, large table, and no nasty kickback problems is ideal for a great variety of sawing applications (Fig. II-1).

Five techniques on the band saw have been chosen for this part:

- A circle jig and plans to make one. The circle jig may be used to make the bottom of the wooden bucket, parts for the round birdhouse, and the carousel.
- Resawing—cutting boards (or shapes) thinner. Resawing is used in making the sides of the jewelry box, and also in cutting the animal shapes in the carousel.
- Pattern sawing—one easy way to cut many parts the same size. Pattern sawing is illustrated in the birdhouse plans, but this technique may be used in many projects.
- Split ring construction—a way to make hollow shapes and bowls on the band saw. This technique is used to develop economical bowl blanks for the wood lathe, and also for preparing blanks for carving and abrasive sanding. It is a wonderful technique to explore, because each new application leads to more project ideas!
- Cutting green wood cylinders. This is introduced in six project ideas: the round canister, dough tray, curved treasure chest, piggy bank, round birdhouse, and plant holder. Take a piece of green wood from the wood pile, and make an inventory of curved parts for all sorts of future projects.

Fig. II-1. Band saw (Courtesy Delta).

5
Circle Jig

THE BAND SAW CAN BE EASILY ADAPTED TO CUT NEAR PERFECT CIRCLES WITH
a circle jig (Fig. 5-1). Circle jigs pivot the stock around a central pin. The
stock is rotated through the band saw blade. The pin is sometimes replaced by a
dowel if the part has a hole in the center, such as a toy wheel that has an axle
hole, or a clock face with a hole for the clock shaft. Whatever the pin arrangement, the jig has these advantages:

- It is easily made with materials on hand.
- It is easy to store and set up.
- It can be adjustable to different circle radii, and accept stock larger than
  the circle diameter.
- It provides a way to find the center of a blank without extra layout work.

The jig shown here will do these things, and with its plywood table, is easy
to adapt for other special features. The jig is built around a plywood table, which
should be a few inches larger than the band saw table. Fashion the jig as shown in
the plans. The miter gauge stick beneath the table should fit snugly in the band
saw table slot without sticking. Machine the dovetail slot and stick, using either a
router or table saw.

Slide the jig on the band saw table and cut the plywood until the blade is
lined up 90 degrees with the pin in any position. This step is important to ensure
the band saw blade tracks correctly around the circle. Secure the stop underneath
the jig so that the jig may only slide until it reaches this point.

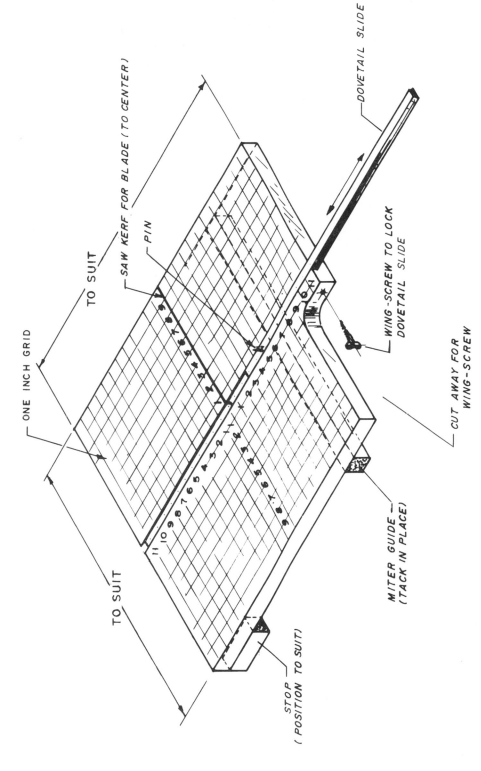

Fig. 5-1. Circle jig for use with band saw.

117

Fig. 5-2. Set the radius pin, move the jig into the band saw, and rotate the wood through the blade.

Lay out a grid in the plywood with the zero point at the tip of the band saw blade. This will allow quick centering of odd shaped pieces put on the jig. It will also be a rule for setting the length of the radius. The table plywood is sawn out with the band saw and a wing screw placed so that the slide may be locked in any position.

To use the jig, set the pin at the required circle radius and lock it in place. Place stock on the jig pin, using the grid to locate the center of the stock. The stock may be larger than the circle diameter, provided it will clear the band saw case when it is rotated (Fig. 5-2).

Turn the saw on and slide the jig forward until it reaches its stop. Now rotate the stock around the pin. When the circle is complete and the waste removed, slide the jig back to load the next piece (Fig. 5-3).

If the band saw tracks inside the circle, or tends to wander to the outside, move the stop under the plywood table slightly forward or backward to compensate for the wander. This adjustment will change the pin relationship to the front of the band saw blade.

Fig. 5-3. Completed circle.

6
Resawing

THE BAND SAW IS AN ABLE-BODIED MACHINE THAT WILL SAW CURVES, RIP straight lines, crosscut, bevel, cut all sorts of jointwork, and resaw. It is the saw of choice for furniture makers, and should be the first machine the novice woodworker buys. In the projects in this book, the band saw is used to resaw the animal parts of the carousel, to slice thin the sides of the treasure chest, jewelry box, and candy dish. The round green cylinders used in the round canister, dough tray, plant holder, curved treasure chest, and piggy bank are all resawn on the band saw.

Resawing is defined as slicing thinner boards from thicker ones. I liberally include sawing of green cylinders in this category, although this process does not include the use of a fence, and the cut is, of course, on a curve.

Two woodworkers of the same skill level may have very different results and opinions after their first efforts at resawing. One may be delighted with his/her efforts, the other ready to give it up for good. Even if they used the same band saw, their results may not be the same. The difficulty with resawing is that there are plenty of variables affecting each person's efforts. Fortunately, all those variables are easy to track down and manipulate, improving the results.

There are so many band saws on the market, old and new, that it is impractical to compare them. An erroneous assumption is that a new machine is set up and adjusted correctly. In too many cases, this is not so. Simply stated, all that is required is for a sharp blade to go wisking powerfully past the table, nice and true, without deflection or vibration. Make all adjustments with this in mind.

First check the band saw for vibration as it is running. If it vibrates, track down the source—whether it be the motor, belt, pulley, or wheels out of balance—and correct the difficulty. The band saw wheels may be wobbling, or worse, out of round. Out-of-round wheels may tension the blade, then slack it, leading to horrible cutting results. Once the vibration is corrected, tension the blade correctly. I favor tensioning on the high side, especially when resawing (Fig. 6-1).

Check that the blade is tracking correctly on the wheels, then check the upper and lower guide assemblies. The upper and lower guide blocks are there to keep the blade from deflecting side to side. Thrust bearings in back of the blade keep the saw blade from bowing backward during the cut. They should be in light

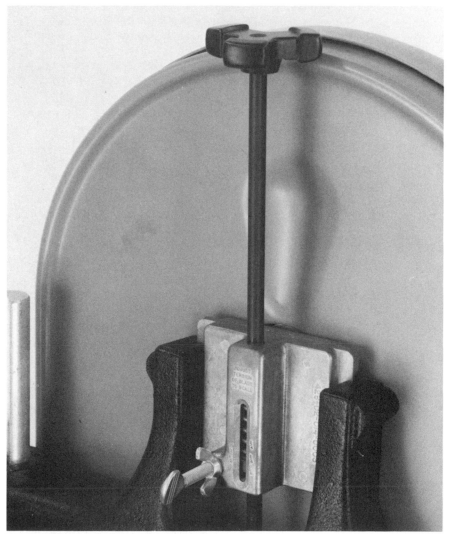

Fig. 6-1. Tension adjustment (Courtesy Delta).

contact with the blade as it tracks correctly. The guide blocks should be very close to the blade but not touching or deflecting the blade as it travels from the top wheel to the bottom drive wheel (Fig. 6-2).

Check this adjustment as the upper guide arm is raised and lowered, the full extent of its travel. The guide blocks are there to steady the blade but not to bend or deflect it. Dig out the owner's manual and correct these adjustments, if necessary.

Now the band saw is running smoothly, the tension is correct, and the guide assemblies are adjusted properly, it is time to check that the table is set 90 degrees to the blade. Check this with a square on the table both beside the blade and in front of the blade. Move the table and reset the pointer back to 0 degrees, if necessary (Figs. 6-3 and 6-4).

Band saws set for constant resawing use wide blades with as few as 3 to 4 teeth per inch. The widely spaced teeth provide plenty of chip clearance and the wide blade is more stable and resistant to bowing back than a narrow one. How-

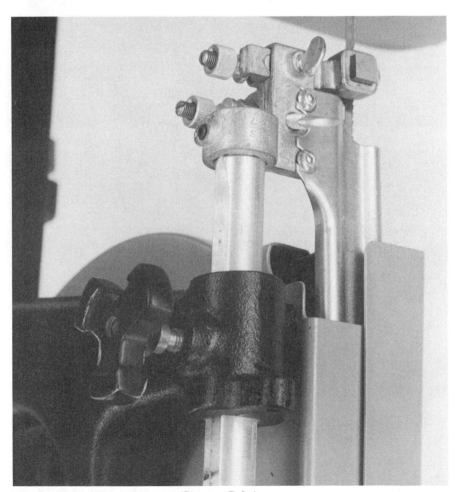

Fig. 6-2. Guide block adjustment (Courtesy Delta).

Fig. 6-3. Adjust table square to blade (Courtesy Delta).

ever, occasional resawing may be accomplished with blades as narrow as $3/8$ or $1/4$ inch, provided the teeth do not exceed 6 teeth per inch and the blade tracks successfully through the stock. The band saw blade itself is the most important component in successful resawing. Some blades track straight, others tend to drift left or right. Blades that track left or right make resawing slightly more difficult, but are by no means impossible to work with. They do not track straight

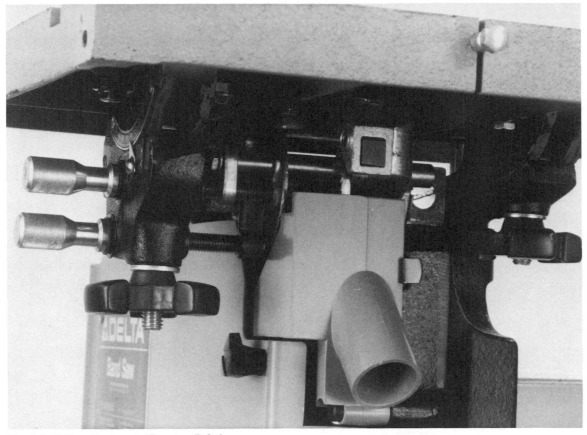

Fig. 6-4. Table adjustments (Courtesy Delta).

because the set of the saw teeth is unbalanced left to right, or the teeth on one side of the set are sharper than those of the other side. This condition, although irritating, is not uncommon with band saw blades.

Resawing is best done using steel blades or bimetal blades. Carbide-tipped blades, also commonly available, are not as desirable on small machines because they use more power with their thick kerf, and are much more expensive. Bimetal blades, made from two metals welded together, seem to have the edge in resawing. They are made with tough teeth (high-speed cobalt steel) and carbon steel back. They may be tensioned higher, and consequently bow and wobble less than the same size steel blade. As may be expected, bimetal blades cost two to three times more than steel, but last longer.

Resawing may be done freehand, with a straight fence, or with a point fence. The best way to practice resawing and to check blade drift is to resaw freehand (Fig. 6-5). Choose wide stock that is low to the table. Scribe several lines close together down the top of the stock. Safely guide the stock past the blade, slicing thin sections off. Check and see if the blade wanders to the left or right. By angling the stock into the blade, it is possible to compensate for the drift of the

124

blade and get a feel for this type of cutting. Tall thin stock, such as a wide board on edge, is not suitable for freehand resawing. The blade might suddenly exit through the side of the stock if the board is tilted. A fence is needed for this type of resawing.

Often a straight fence is fashioned for resawing (Fig. 6-6). The fence supplied with the saw is usually too low. A wooden fence should be made that is taller and sets 90 degrees to the table surface. The straight fence is made with a base extending to one side that provides a good clamping surface. With a little experimentation, the fence can be clamped to the table in an angle that compensates for the natural drift of the blade. Once this arrangement is set up, repeated veneers or thin boards may be resawn from a wide board.

The point fence shown in Fig. 6-7 is simple, and it allows the operator to steer the wood through the cut. The round nose of the fence or point must be clamped to the table at a position 90 degrees to the blade teeth tips. The point may be positioned close to the blade, allowing thin veneers to be resawn. In this type of cutting, a line (or lines) is scribed in the top edge of the stock. This line is split with the blade as the stock is resawn. The stock is gently pushed up against the point fence with a push stick during the cut. Practice and experience produce resawn boards with consistent thickness. Soon you will be using the band saw for resawing as much as contour cutting.

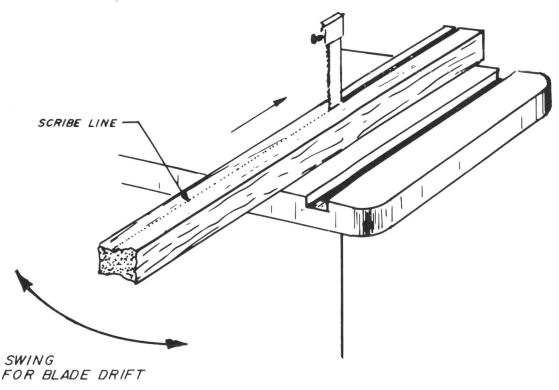

Fig. 6-5. Sawing freehand.

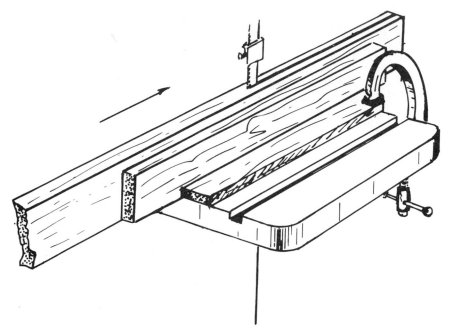

Fig. 6-6. Sawing with a straight fence.

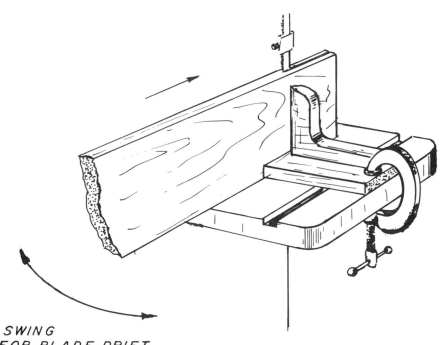

SWING
FOR BLADE DRIFT

Fig. 6-7. Sawing with a point fence.

Fig. 6-8. Carousel.

Project 11: Carousel

This toy carousel is a joy to make (Fig. 6-8). It winds up around the center pole, then gravity forces the carriage to wind down and up the other direction. It changes direction again and repeats the motion for up to a minute. This one is fashioned with brightly colored satin ribbon and flashy flags that my children glued on the carousel.

The project consists of a round base and carousel disk, a few dowels, band sawn animals, and some ribbon. The disks may be cut using the band saw circle jig, and the horses are resawn from a single block of wood (Table 6-1).

Start by cutting the base disk and the carousel disk. Most woods will work, although the base should be a dense and heavy wood. Locate the center of each disk (the band saw jig will leave a nail mark at the center) and drill holes for the

Table 6-1. Materials List. Carousel.

NO.	NAME	SIZE	REQ'D.
1	BASE	3/4 X 5 DIA.	1
2	PLATFORM	1/2 X 7 1/2 DIA.	1
3	CENTER POLE	5/16 DIA. X 12 LONG	1
4	CAP	5/8 DIA. X 3/4 LONG	1
5	HORSE	3/8 X 2 1/2 - 4 LONG	4
6	POST	1/8 DIA. - 3 1/2 LG.	4
7	FLAG POLE	1/8 DIA. - 1 1/4 LONG	1
8	FLAG	1/2 X 1 3/4 LONG	5
9	TWINE - COLORED	1/16 DIA. - 26 LONG	2
10	TRIM - COLORED	1/16 DIA. - 24 LONG	1

dowel. The base hole should fit the dowel snugly. The carousel hole is larger, so that it fits (and spins) loosely over the center dowel (Figs. 6-9 and 6-10).

The horses are cut on the band saw. Lay a pattern on a thick block and cut out the silhouette of the horse. Then slice each individual horse from the master block (Fig. 6-11). Notice the block of wood underneath the horse being resawn. It supports the small feet of the horse, keeping it from falling in the band saw throat plate. You can choose many different animals to put on your carousel besides horses.

Locate the holes in the carousel disk and drill for the horse mounts and the string locations. The 1/8-inch holes through the horses should be drilled on the drill press with a fence supporting the horse parallel to the bit. The side of each horse is sanded, but the edges may be left rough to simulate the horses' mane. Glue and mount the horses in place.

Notch the center dowel in the top end to accept the satin ribbon. The cap covering the notched end is made from a 5/8-inch dowel. Wedge the top cap in place, so that it may be taken off to level the carousel disk, if necessary.

If the carousel is to be painted or stained, do this before the ribbon is attached. Bright colors and ribbons make the piece attractive. Attach the ribbon last. Knot the end of two ribbons and feed them up through the carousel disk, through the cross notch at the top of the pole, and down through the opposite side of the carousel disk. Adjust the knots at the end of the ribbon so the carousel is level and slightly above the base. Using two different colors makes a nice effect when the carousel winds and unwinds.

Now, wind the carousel up and let it go! Beware: The action of this toy is catching. I spent as much time playing with the carousel as making it.

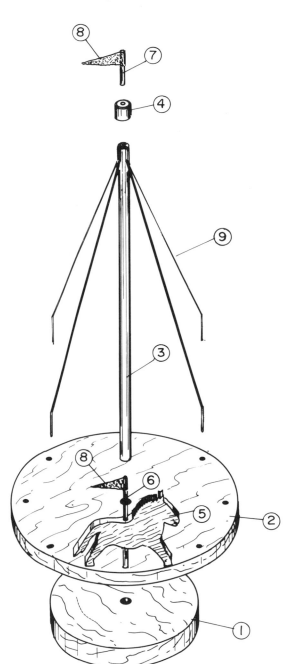

Fig. 6-9. Plans for carousel: Pictorial and top view.

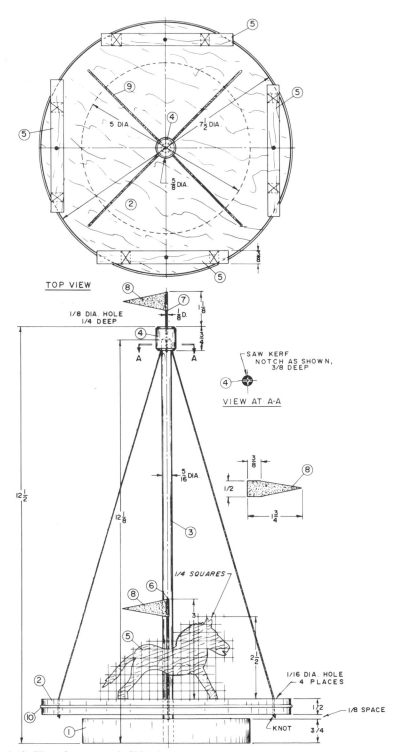

TOP VIEW

1/8 DIA. HOLE
1/4 DEEP

SAW KERF
NOTCH AS SHOWN,
3/8 DEEP

VIEW AT A-A

1/4 SQUARES

1/16 DIA. HOLE
4 PLACES

1/8 SPACE

KNOT

Fig. 6-10. Plans for carousel: Side view.

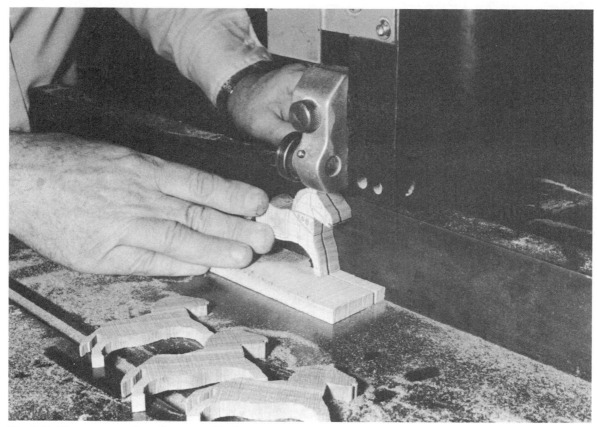

Fig. 6-11. Horses resawn from the master block.

7
Pattern Sawing

PATTERN SAWING, ESPECIALLY WITH THE BAND SAW, IS A GOOD WAY TO CUT OUT identical multiple parts. A fine example of this technique is the birdhouse plans that follow. The pattern sawing jig is designed for straight-sided parts, and the pattern is identical in size to the finished part. The parts need not be rectangular nor square, so long as there are no parts concave to the shape.

The pattern saw jig consists of a plywood fence—simply the edge of a piece of plywood—suspended above the table and in line with the blade. The pattern is stacked on top of the blank and rides along the fence. The waste wood is cut off one side of the blank below. Then the pattern is rotated and another side of the blank sliced off. The pattern and blank are usually held together by two small brads driven through the pattern and tacked into the blank. Each time the pattern is set on a new blank, the brad points hold the blank steady under the pattern during the cuts.

To make the jig, first cut out the patterns, which are identical in size to the finished part. Attach a handle to each part—a section of broom handle is adequate—far enough from the edge so that the handles will not strike the upper guide assembly of the band saw during the cut. Large parts that hang over the edge of the table may not need handles on the patterns. Drive several small brads through the pattern to grip the blank. If brad holes are objectional in the blank, try double-faced tape. It will need changing occasionally, but will leave no marks.

Now cut a piece of plywood to cover half the band saw table. The edge of the plywood that the pattern rides against must be a straight edge. Cut a small notch in the straight edge to house the band saw blade. The jig will be positioned so that the band saw kerf (outside) and the straight edge are in line.

Clamp the plywood to the band saw table so that it is suspended slightly higher than the thickness of the blanks. This height will allow clearance for the waste sections and a good surface for the pattern to ride against. A strip of wood the length of the band saw table, 2 inches wide and slightly thicker than the blank stock will do. Clamp the strip under the plywood as far to the left as you can. Allow plenty of space for waste under the table. Adjust the jig so that the band saw blade comes as close to the pattern as possible without touching it. If the pattern is shaved with each cut it will wear smaller, and the parts will become progressively smaller as well.

Once the pattern sawing jig is in operation, there is no layout work to be done. The pattern is set on the blank and pushed along the fence, rotated and pushed again until the pattern and blank are identical. The simplicity and safety of jig are ideal when working with children or the disabled (with proper supervision). However, certain additional safety measures help in these cases: First move the top guide assembly as low to the plywood as possible. Make sure the band saw blade is totally covered above the plywood fence. A piece of plexiglass may be fashioned to cover the guide blocks and secured to the top guide assembly. The only blade exposure is below the plywood fence.

Project 12: Birdhouse

This birdhouse is a perfect project to try out the band saw pattern sawing technique. The birdhouse was first developed for young people in the 4-H program (Fig. 7-1). Children could cut out parts for a birdhouse and assemble it in a very short time, thus promoting interest in woodworking.

Cutting and assembly of the birdhouse is straightforward. Once the parts are cut the project is nailed and glued together. Either the roof or the bottom is screwed on to provide clean-out access (Table 7-1).

Here are some pointers concerning the birdhouse:

- If young children are to nail the birdhouse together, make the parts thicker than 1/4 inch. Beginners find it difficult to keep the nails from coming out the side.
- Size the entry hole according to the intended occupant. Remember a large hole invites a predator to stop by for lunch. The size of the entry hole will determine the kinds of birds the house attracts.
- Plan how the birdhouse is to be mounted. If, for example, the birdhouse will be attached to a porch railing, the top may be screwed on after the birdhouse is fastened to the railing through the bottom.

Figure 7-2 shows all the parts of the birdhouse and their respective patterns. Notice the patterns are the same size as the parts. Handles (broomstick sections) have been screwed to the patterns to make them easy to push through the saw.

Fig. 7-1. Birdhouse.

Table 7-1. Materials List: Birdhouse.

NO.	NAME	SIZE	REQ'D.
I	FRONT / BACK	1/4 X 6 3/4 - 8 LG.	2
2	SIDE	1/4 X 5 - 5 LONG	2
3	BASE	1/4 X 4 - 6 1/4 LG.	I
4	ROOF - RIGHT	1/4 X 5 1/2-7 LG.	I
5	ROOF - LEFT	1/4 X 5 3/4 - 7 LG.	I
G	ROOST	1/4 DIA. - 2 LG.	I

Figure 7-3 illustrates the pattern sawing jig, one pattern, and a part ready to be cut. Notice that the pattern sawing jig is a piece of plywood with a good straight edge. It is suspended over the table, high enough to allow the stock to slide underneath and the pattern to ride against it. The straight edge is notched, allowing the band saw blade to run just a hair inside the straight edge. That way the pattern is never cut. Suspend the jig over the table by placing a spacer block

Fig. 7-2. Pattern layout and parts.

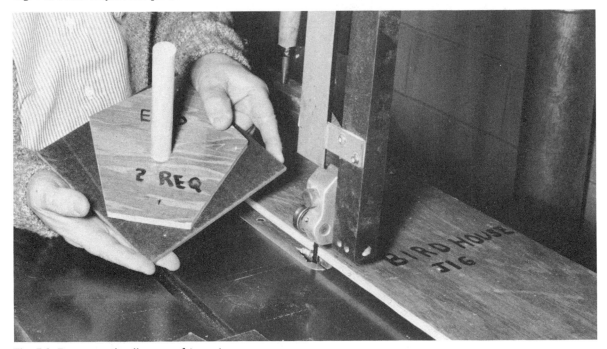

Fig. 7-3. Pattern sawing jig secured to part.

underneath the right hand edge and clamping this affair to the band saw table. Make the jig as wide as possible between the spacer block and the blade, to allow plenty of room for waste (Figs. 7-4 and 7-5).

Push the pattern, with the stock underneath, past the saw blade, turn, and cut again until all sides are trimmed. To hold the stock in place and prevent it from shifting during the cut, drive two brad points through the pattern from the top.

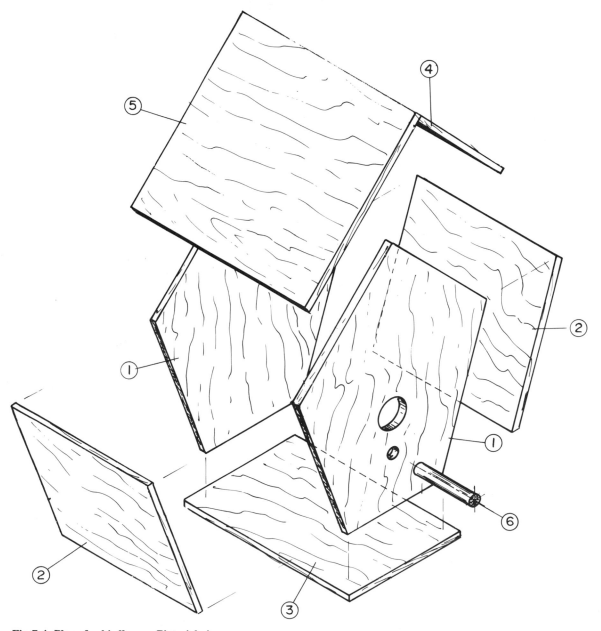

Fig 7-4. Plans for birdhouse: Pictorial view.

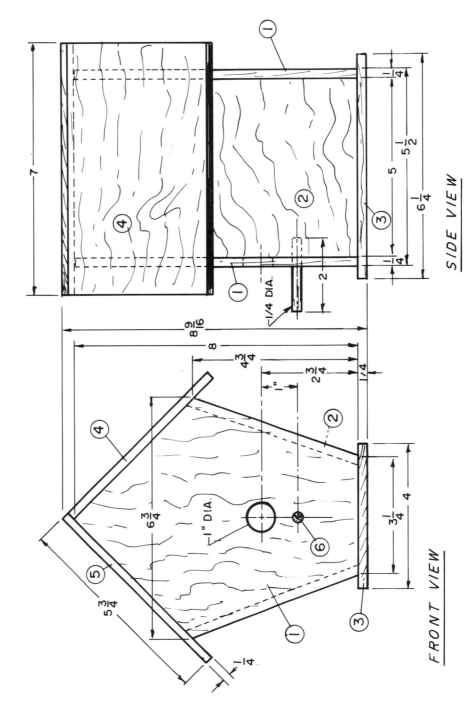

SIDE VIEW

FRONT VIEW

Fig. 7-5. Plans for birdhouse: Front and side views.

137

Fig. 7-6. Each part is sawn.

Fig. 7-7. The part is separated from the pattern.

138

The stock may also be held in place with sandpaper glued underneath the pattern, or with double-faced tape (Fig. 7-6).

The new part is separated from the pattern, and you are ready to go again. You can turn out 10 parts per minute (Fig. 7-7).

The advantages of pattern sawing is obvious in mass production techniques. It also offers a unique opportunity for visually impaired people, children, or people with motor skill problems because the pattern may be fitted on the stock by feel, or by a box loading system. Attach a plexiglass guard to the top guide post and the blade is covered down to the plywood jig. Only the blade below the plywood is exposed, making the operation as safe as possible.

8

Split Ring
Construction

THERE ARE SO MANY USES FOR A FINE WOODEN BOWL. THEY MAY BE USED for serving salad, displaying dry flowers, or as fruit bowls. We consider the bowls themselves a form of artwork, and I am infatuated with split ring construction.

Split rings have become my favorite method of bowl blank construction. I started using this technique years ago to economize wood supplies. Since then, I have invented numerous variations in sizes, shapes, colors, and patterns. A 12-inch diameter bowl can be made with 1 board foot of stock. Even a bowl with a lid and knob can be made from less than 2 board feet. I often use scraps of other projects. What started as sensible Yankee frugality, eventually evolved into a rich inventory of interesting bowls. Simple techniques can produce an astonishing variety—all with scraps from the corner!

Project 13: Split Ring Bowls

Split ring bowls are all made from half rings, cut from two boards. I call these boards *ring boards*. Half rings are cut from each board on the band saw, with the table tilted to 45 degrees. The rings are glued together and eventually stacked into a hollow bowl shape. The glued bowl blank is hollow and turns quickly, more than compensating for the time it takes to cut and glue the rings. Although the walls of the blank are only $3/4$ inch thick, graceful cyma curves, rims, and feet are possible (Fig. 8-1).

Fig. 8-1. Split ring bowls.

The variety of bowls is possible because of the constantly varying shape, color, and joint patterns. The bowl blank itself is spartan, with straight sides that splay out at 45 degrees from a flat bottom. After the blank is trued, I work to a shape. If the outer ring is cut at 90 degrees, the outside of the bowl will have a thick rim. I turn a bowl that has curved sides and feet with a downturned rim. This rim shape makes the bowl easy to carry and hold. The depth of the bowl is controlled by the number of ring layers used. One ring (over the bottom) makes a good platter. Two rings make the bowl great for holding your pocket contents or an evening's share of popcorn. Three rings deepen the bowl at the expense of the bottom size, although you might want to experiment by gluing the bottom to a platter blank as a base (Fig. 8-2).

The simple beauty is enriched by mixing different color and textured woods. The most basic contrast is made by cutting the rings from two ring boards of different woods. The half rings will be different colors, the full rings can be rotated and stacked in different configurations.

Rings cut from laminated boards carry straight strips that give the illusion of bending, depending on how the bowl is held. Once I chanced on a rejected batch of laminated cutting boards. They were laminated from cherry, walnut, maple, and oak, with purple heart stripes. Stacking the rings in different directions used all the cutting boards without a single clone. The colors of those bowls were absolutely spectacular.

Pattern is accomplished by choosing different joint work between the rings. Cut the joint between the two ring boards before the half rings are cut. Each ring

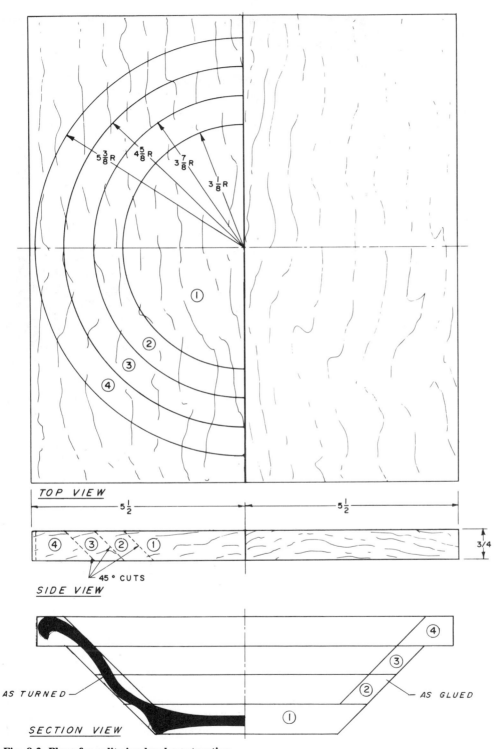

Fig. 8-2. Plans for split ring bowl construction.

layer reflects that joint in the finished bowl. The simple butt joint draws straight lines alternately down the bowl. Scarf joints slash the bowl with diagonal lines. Tongue-and-groove, sliding dovetail, and even a glue joint cutter all add distinctive pattern with little effort (Fig. 8-3).

A recent discovery of mine is the multiple dovetail pattern, which has become quite a conversation piece. Each of the ring boards is made with three or more sliding dovetail sections of contrasting wood. The joint between the ring boards is also a sliding dovetail. The end result is a multiple dovetail pattern in each ring.

How is the dovetail in the bottom of the bowl made? That interesting pattern is not a dovetail at all, but is made by cutting halfway through the bottom sliding dovetail. If this dovetail pattern is cut in the bottom of the bowl and repeated on the underside, it's hard to detect how the bowl was glued up.

Although lathe turning is the usual method of shaping, some blanks could be abrasively shaped or carved. The blank is nearly the finished shape, ideally suited to shaping by abrasion, disks, flappers, or sandblasting. I cut rejects—those with a bad ring—smaller on the band saw and sanded them into small candy dishes and other shapes. Some bowls were shaped, drilled with holes, then fitted with macrame cord and hung as plant holders. Hanging plants grow out and

Fig. 8-3. Dovetail and scarf bowls.

down through the holes. These are excellent for small gifts. Except for an occasional bad bottom and the corner ring board scraps, nothing goes to waste in my shop anymore.

Making the Blank

1. Choose two 3/4-inch boards and lay them side by side on the workbench. They must be the same thickness, but can be different species of wood. The two boards together should measure a square that will be the diameter of the finished bowl. Check the capacity or turning radius of your lathe first. Then prepare a good glue joint between the boards. Use a butt joint at first, and later try the scarf joint or dovetail joint.

2. Locate the center and draw the largest circle possible in the blank (Fig. 8-4). Tape the boards together. Now draw smaller circles around the same center, decreasing the radius 3/4 inch each time. You will end up with two or three rings 3/4 inch apart around the bottom.

3. Separate the ring boards and cut the rings out on the band saw (Fig. 8-5). The outside ring is cut with the table 90 degrees to the blade (Fig.

Fig. 8-4. Locate center, draw the largest circle possible.

144

Fig. 8-5. Ring boards are separated.

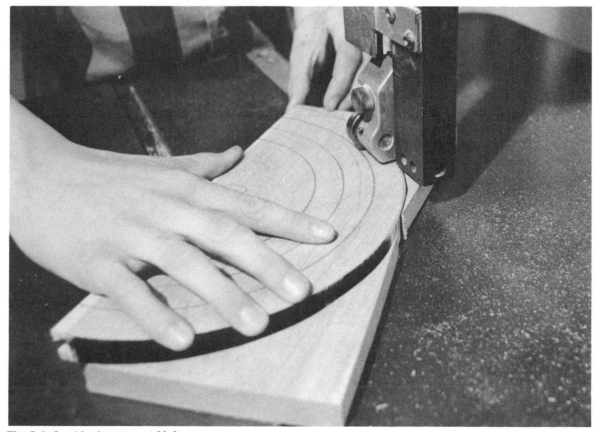

Fig. 8-6. Outside ring sawn at 90 degrees.

8-6). All other rings are cut with the band saw table tilted to 45 degrees (Fig. 8-7). Cutting the rings out with the table at 45 degrees takes a little practice, but before long you will be an expert. Tilt the band saw table to 45 degrees and stand on the downward side of the table during the cut. Stay on the line because you need a thick walled bowl to turn or shape later (Fig. 8-8).

4. Glue all the half rings together (Fig. 8-9). Gentle pressure from a clamp or even hand pressure will do the trick. Be sure to keep the half rings aligned properly. Yellow carpenter's glue is excellent for the task. Set aside for a few hours.

5. Next, glue the rings into a stack upside down. First, sand any glue ridge or misalignment off the rings. Stack the rings upside down and check the contact areas between the rings. Rotate the rings so the glue joints are staggered and the best grain pattern appears. Mark down the stack with a pencil so they can be restacked the same way. When satisfied, glue the rings together and clamp the stack down to the table. Keep the rings centered.

6. From here the bowl blank may be carved, fluted, abrasively sanded, sandblasted, or turned on the lathe.

Fig. 8-7. Other rings cut at 45 degrees.

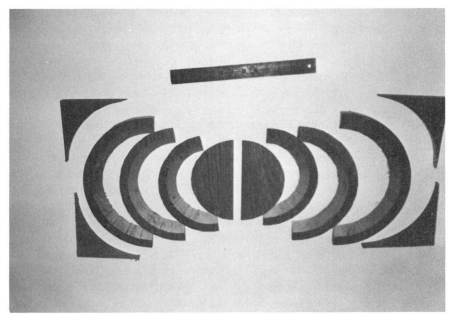

Fig. 8-8. Ring segments and corner waste blocks.

Fig. 8-9. Glue the half rings together.

I turn my bowl blanks on the lathe. Mount the bowl on the lathe with screws. Glue a plywood disk and paper back to the bowl blank in one operation when the ring stack is first glued. After the assembly is dried, use a screwgun and short drywall screws to mount the faceplate. This step, fast and quick, usually requires that the faceplate be redrilled with smaller holes to accept drywall screws. Drywall screws have low shear strength, so use at least four screws. The paper glued between the plywood disk and bowl will allow easy parting when it's time to turn the bottom. The bowl must be centered; any measure off center will double as the bowl rotates.

After unsuccessfully experimenting with elaborate jigs to center the faceplate, I simply opted for the guesswork method. First attach the faceplate with two screws, estimating the center. Pencil a line around the faceplate onto the plywood disk. Mount the bowl on the lathe. With the power off, rotate the bowl by hand and mark the high and low spots by holding a pencil on the tool rest. Note the difference between high and low. Move the faceplate half the difference toward the high side. Reattach with all screws. The bowl will be centered.

I shape the outside with a gouge, then switch to a roundnose scraper for inside work. A roundnose scraper is ground with the burr left on. The handle of the tool is slightly above center and the tool tip below center. Therefore, the burr will shave the wood, keeping end grain tear and subsequent sanding to a minimum. After the burr wears, touch it up on a waterstone several times before regrinding the tool. If the bowl is turned with sharp tools and minimum grain tear, it is faster to hand sand the bowl than to sand it on the lathe.

Once the inside and outside of the bowl is finished, turn to the underside. Secure the bowl to a plywood disk with double-faced tape and gently cut the feet. The underside should be left concave so that the bowl will sit level. Mount a reuseable plywood disk to the lathe and true it. I use an outboard faceplate and mount it to the back of the lathe. Then draw a series of concentric circles in the plywood with a dark pencil while the plywood is spinning. The dark lines show through the double-faced tape, enabling the bowl to be centered. The downturned rim provides an adequate surface area for tape adhesion. Even so, I cut gently with my hand on the bowl and use a face shield. Each bowl blank takes about an hour to turn, excluding gluing the blank.

Lids and knobs are easy additions. Usually a lid is a two-ring blank, shaped to fit a rabbet groove turned in the bowl rim (Figs. 8-10 and 8-11). Both the bowl and lid blanks are mounted on individual faceplates and trued. Mark the location of the rabbet groove on the bowl rim area and cut. Then turn the bowl, but leave attached to the faceplate. Turn the bowl feet only after the lid is finished. Next, turn the lid to fit tightly in the bowl groove.

Part the lid from its faceplate and wedge tightly into the mounted bowl, then tape in place. Now it is possible to turn the knob. A recessed knob may be turned in the lid bottom. If raised knobs are preferred, add an extra scrap of wood between the lid and the faceplate assembly. (Waste from the corner of the ring board is excellent for this.) After the lid is turned, remove the tape. Now the bowl may be parted from the faceplate and taped to the plywood disk, and the underside turned.

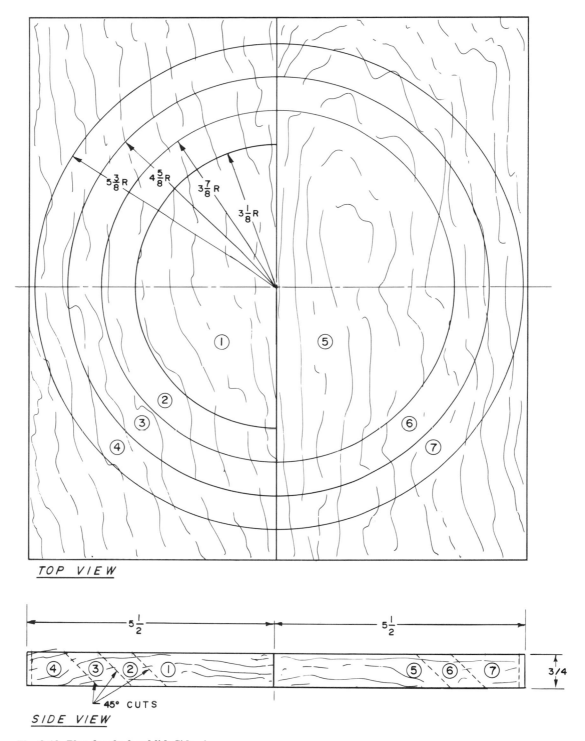

TOP VIEW

SIDE VIEW

45° CUTS

Fig. 8-10. Plan for the bowl lid: Side view.

149

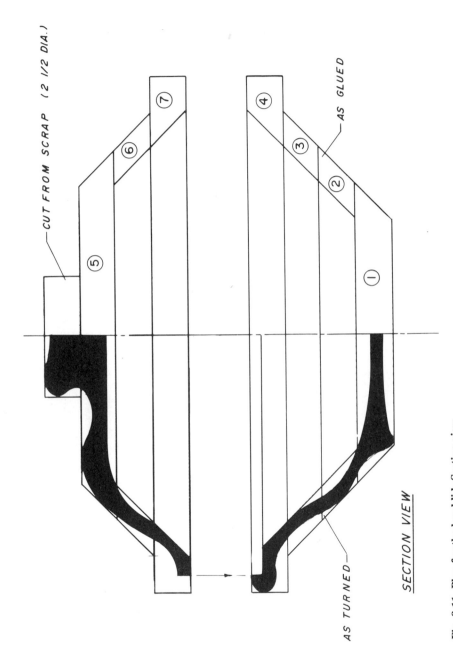

Fig. 8-11. Plan for the bowl lid: Section view.

9

Drying Green Cylinders in the Round

ONE FINE FALL DAY, WHILE LYING ON THE WOOD PILE LISTENING TO THE beetles chew the oak beneath me, I began to think about drying wood in the round. How could I make a birdhouse, canister, planter, jewelry box, or bud vase out of those chunks of green butternut? Within four weeks, with the addition of several scraps of flat stock, I had finished projects. The process of cutting and drying green cylinders, described here, I call drying in the round (Fig. 9-1).

As a beginning woodturner, I often practiced on green stock from the wood pile (green wood refers to any wood above the fiber saturation point). Turning green wood produces a smooth, gleaming finish. This, however, does not last. Within minutes the moisture on the wood evaporates and a few hours later, deep checks develop. Checks, which enlarge into cracks, are the result of the wood relieving itself of the stress generated by uneven shrinkage during drying.

It was this checking, radially increasing from the center, that first prompted me to core a round branch section and observe what happens when the outside cylinder dries. I cut the first cylinders on the lathe, mounted with the end grain attached to a faceplate. I turned the round section outside with a tail stock support and then cut inside as deeply as possible. What was left was a cylinder with both ends removed. I sealed the end grain of the cylinders and then set them aside to dry. When dry, I turned the cylinders as I would in a glued-up stave construction.

Fig. 9-1. Green cylinder projects.

Project 14: Cutting Cylinders

The process of cutting cylinders on the lathe has limited advantages. Cylinders can be made seamless for special canisters or clock frames, but this requires more labor and is wasteful of stock. Later, I developed ways of cutting multiple cylinders from the same section using the band saw and settled for one glued seam.

I have experimented with many native hardwoods, including butternut, red oak, sumac, apple, black cherry, and birch with equal success. The cylinders dry quickly, without cracking, in about a month. The drying time will vary, depending on relative humidity, temperature, air circulation, wall thickness, and species. The cylinders are weighed after cutting and periodically thereafter. When the weight of the cylinder stabilizes, it has reached equilibrium moisture content (EMC) and can be used. Final drying should take place in the same type of environment as that in which the wood will be used.

The cylinders can be cut from any non-resinous wood that has not cracked. With a little practice, it will take less than 10 minutes to cut and glue each cylinder, and therefore it will be easy to build up a stock for future use. I have made canisters, clock frames, wall sconces, planters, mail boxes, bread trays, lamps, jewelry boxes, bud vases, and many parts for larger pieces from these cheap and inexpensive sources of round stock. All that is required is green stock, a sturdy band saw, glue, and a clamping arrangement.

The maximum height and width of each cylinder is limited by the capacity of the band saw. As the round stock is placed upright on the band saw table, the maximum length of each cylinder may only reach the cutting height capacity of the band saw. I frequently start with a large cylinder 11 inches long and up to a foot in diameter, cut on a 20-inch saw. It is best, however, to experiment with cutting techniques on smaller stock. *Caution*: Small, underpowered three-wheeled band saws with their thin blades are not equal to the task.

Choose green stock as round as possible and with the pith centered. This is important if the cylinder is to be eventually turned on the lathe and you want the cylinder to dry round. Stay away from resinous woods; they will gum up everything. Square the ends so that the stock sits upright on the band saw table without rocking (Fig. 9-2). I use a V-block with a miter gauge for this purpose. On the top end, use a compass and draw the largest circle possible inside the bark layer. Using the same center, draw a second circle inside the first. The wall thickness between the circles may vary with the intended use of the cylinder. After some research on the different radial and tangential shrinkage, I usually settle for $1/2$-inch wall thickness, which doesn't take long to dry. Continue to draw smaller circles until you reach the minimum curve the band saw blade will negotiate (Fig. 9-3).

Check the band saw; the guide locks or bearings and the blade tension should be accurately adjusted. A dull blade with poor tooth set will only frustrate attempts to cut the cylinder, so this might be a good time for a new blade. I prefer a $1/4$-inch skip tooth blade to negotiate the curves. The table should be freshly

Fig. 9-2. Steady logs with blocks on the band saw.

Fig. 9-3. Draw circles on the end grain.

waxed and set at 90 degrees to the blade. The stock will rotate on the table during the cut, and a rough or sticky table will ruin your accuracy.

Position the stock upright on the band saw table, on the side of the blade that allows comfortable handling. The scarf line tends to slide by under clamping, so enter each circle circumference as a radius line and then swing to a tangent line. This results in a slightly concave entry cut, which will ease clamping problems (Fig. 9-4).

A little experimentation will soon yield good results. Use a push stick nearest the blade to give good control and for safety (Fig. 9-5). Enter the stock into the first circle, carefully cut around until the entry point is past, then shut the band saw down and back the blade out. In some woods, the saw kerf must be gently pried apart to facilitate blade removal. Once the stock is free of the blade, slide the outside cylinder off. I usually cut two or three cylinders after the bark cylinder is cut (Figs. 9-6 and 9-7).

Glue and save the outside bark cylinder; they make excellent birdhouses. I soak the core in water until I can cut a bud vase on the lathe. Right after the bud vase is cut, it must be drilled all the way through its center so it will dry without checking. After drying, the hole is plugged.

After the cylinders are cut they must be glued. Don't leave cylinders overnight; they will move so much that forcing the kerf line back will usually result in

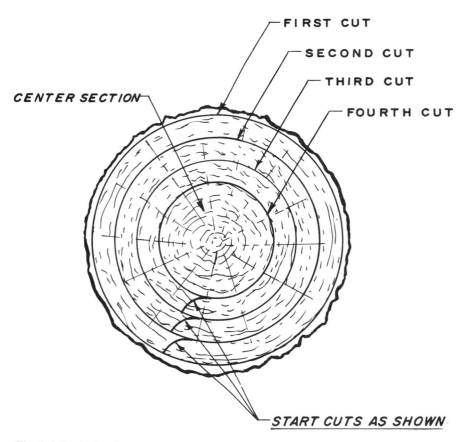

FIRST CUT

SECOND CUT

THIRD CUT

FOURTH CUT

CENTER SECTION

START CUTS AS SHOWN

Fig. 9-4. Beginning the cut.

cracking. I have found large stainless steel worm clamps the easiest clamping method. However, strap clamps, heavy elastics, or inner tube rubber will also work. Glue the saw kerf lines, working the glue in with a piece of stiff cardboard, and then clamp (Fig. 9-8).

Next, coat the end grains of the cylinder with sealer to prevent end grain checking. Weigh each cylinder and record its weight on the cylinder wall and the date it was cut (Fig. 9-9).

The circumference of the cylinder will change quickly as the wood loses moisture. Steel clamps initially applied tightly will slide off with finger pressure the next day, or will have fallen off the cylinders altogether. Drying time will vary considerably depending on relative humidity, temperature, wall thickness, air circulation, and species. The cylinders are safe to use when they reach equilibrium moisture content with the surrounding air. Continue weighing the cylinders periodically, and when the weight stabilizes they are safe to use.

Final drying should take place in the same type of environment the cylinder will eventually be used. This is especially true if the cylinder will be glued to a bottom, which restricts further movement.

Fig. 9-5. Cutting technique.

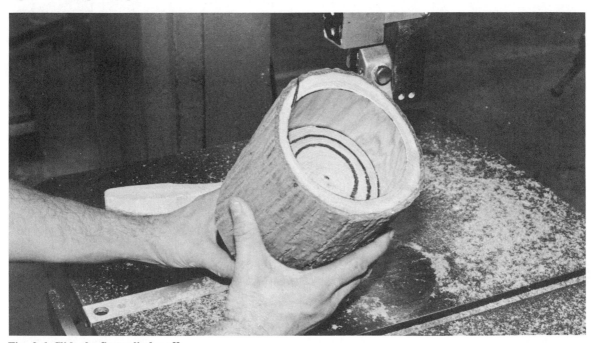

Fig. 9-6. Slide the first cylinder off.

Fig. 9-7. Cylinders from one log section.

Fig. 9-8. Glue and clamp each cylinder together.

Fig. 9-9. Weigh each cylinder and record weight.

For drying, I rope the cylinders overhead out of the way where the air is warm, or sometimes I lay them sideways on a shelf and stack them like a wine rack. With such a cheap supply of native hardwood from the firewood pile or an occasional fallen branch, I constantly find new ways of using these cylinders. This is also a good way to use fruitwoods, which are not normally sawn.

As green wood loses moisture and drops below the fiber saturation point, dimensional changes begin to take place. Wood will decrease in size as it dries. Wood will eventually reach a point where it stabilizes at equilibrium with the surrounding air (EMC). Moisture content (MC) of the wood will slowly continue to adjust with the seasonal changes in humidity. To complicate things a bit, the wood does not lose moisture at the same even rate to its core, nor does it change shape evenly. Most woods will decrease in size during drying about twice as much around the growth rings (tangentially) as across the growth rings toward the center of the tree (radially). The shrinkage along the length of the tree (longitudinally) is not nearly as great (Fig. 9-10).

Also, as a sample is drying, the moisture content will vary in different parts. The outside of the wood and the area near the end grain will dry faster, because moisture travels more quickly toward the end grain than any other direction. As

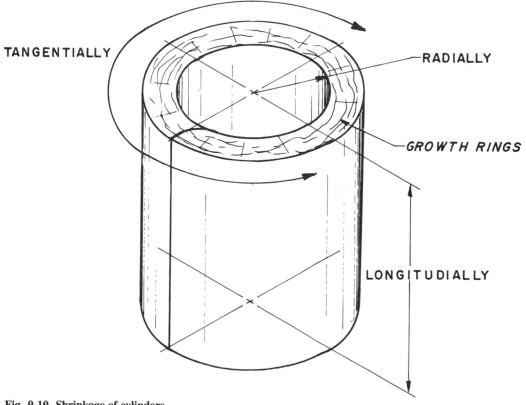

TANGENTIALLY

RADIALLY

GROWTH RINGS

LONGITUDIALLY

Fig. 9-10. Shrinkage of cylinders.

the outside of the wood dries, leaving the inside with a higher moisture content and potentially a larger size, radial and tangential movement produce the cracks, warp, twists, and cup. Wood is hydroscopic, so to some extent it will reabsorb with high humidity and reverse these changes. Woodworkers try to work with stock that has reached equilibrium moisture content and try to anticipate the changes that will take place during seasonal changes of humidity. Today, with our central heating systems, we must anticipate greater dimensional changes than earlier cabinetmakers allowed for.

When green cylinders are cut, glued, and left to dry, they will shrink without cracking, because their shape allows them to move and relieve the drying dimensional changes. The greatest tangential shrinkage around the growth rings can be measured as the decrease of the circumference of the cylinder. The radial shrinkage (which is about half of the tangential change) can be measured by the decrease of the thickness of the cylinder wall. The smallest change is longitudinal and will affect the length of the cylinder. If the cylinder wall is thin enough (this depends on species, but is usually less than 1 inch) and if the end grain is sealed, all three dimensional changes will be relatively independent. The circumference of the cylinder (now without its core) can move independently. The wall thickness and the length of the cylinder can also change its size without restriction.

A cylinder without knots will not crack as it dries. It is interesting to note that a cylinder cut with a knot in the side will usually check around the knot, exactly as the round stock will check and crack if cylinders had not been cut out of it.

Project 15: Round Canister

The round cylinder technique is an excellent way to make a canister, or a matched set of canisters (Figs. 9-11 and 9-12). Each cylinder is cut progressively smaller from the same log, which is perfect for a set. Canisters are turned on the lathe. The canisters illustrated are turned exactly like the stave canister (Fig. 9-11).

Round cylinders show different grain patterns than stave cylinders. The stave cylinder is glued up from many pieces of wood, and shows the grain orientation of each individual piece of wood in the circumference of the cylinder. The round cylinder, on the other hand, exposes grain patterns tangent to the growth rings of the tree, continuous around the circumference. This is quite different from the grain orientation in other projects and presents interesting possibilities. This grain pattern is like a radial veneer, cut similar to a piece of plywood (Fig. 9-13).

Fig. 9-11. Round canister with recessed lid.

Fig. 9-12. Round canister.

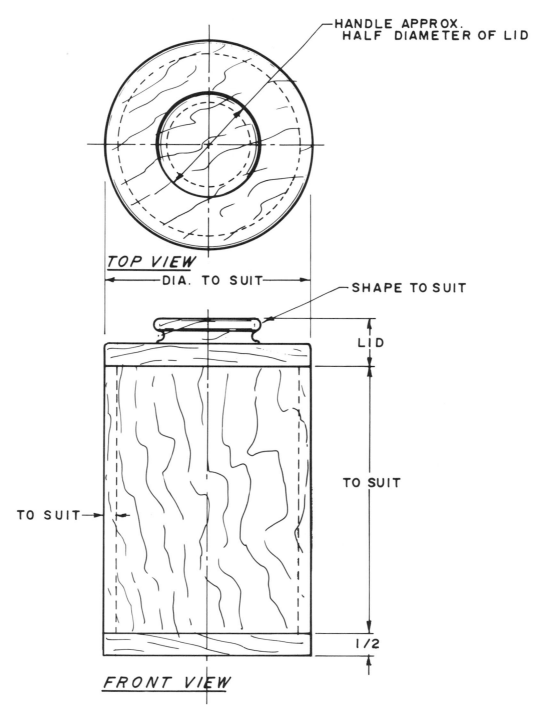

HANDLE APPROX.
HALF DIAMETER OF LID

TOP VIEW
DIA. TO SUIT

SHAPE TO SUIT

LID

TO SUIT

TO SUIT

1/2

FRONT VIEW

Fig. 9-13. Plans for canister.

161

Project 16: Dough Tray

Finally, the right container to show off those delicious bagels or to use for cheese and crackers (Fig. 9-14). Not unlike our little piggy bank, this simple project merely requires cutting a cylinder with the band saw, then halving it. I originally came upon this idea when I broke a cylinder, so don't discard any first foiled attempts at the technique—they can be saved.

Choose the cylinder radius according to the purpose of the tray. Crackers might need a shorter radial cut, while bagels, donuts, or rice cakes could stand the fuller cut of 5- or 6-inch diameter cylinder. For the length, 7 or 8 inches works nicely (Table 9-1).

Halve the cylinder lengthwise on the band saw. Use the band saw fence and support the cylinder from rolling by blocking the underside. The ends will be two pieces of $5/8$-inch stock. To figure the diameter of the ends, take the radius chosen, multiply by 2 and add $3/8$ to $1/2$ inch. Use the drawing to sketch the shape onto the board and with the band saw, cut the rounded shape and the feet (Figs. 9-15 and 9-16).

Using the drill press, you can drill the correct diameter curve that might start and end the handle cutout. Ours uses a $1 1/4$-inch drill hole that is then lined and sawn with a jigsaw. Later the edges are rounded with a router.

Sand and finish all the pieces. Align them. Apply glue and join, checking that the legs are level. Oil the piece with salad bowl finish, and it is ready to use.

Fig. 9-14. Dough tray.

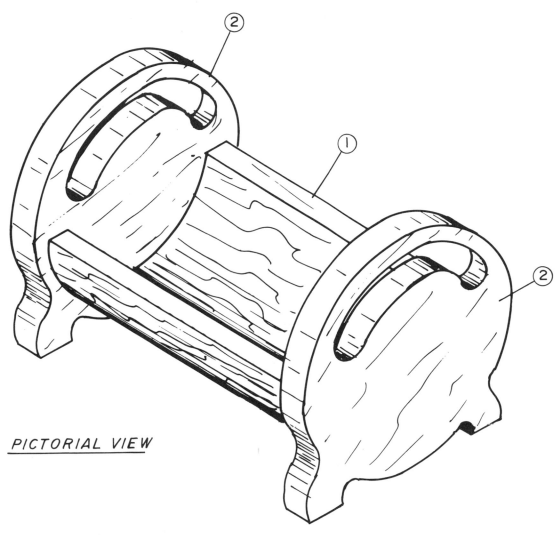

Fig. 9-15. Plans for dough tray: Pictorial.

Table 9-1. Materials List: Dough Tray.

NO.	NAME	SIZE	REQ'D.
1	BODY	5"- 6" DIA./7"- 8" LG.	1
2	END	5/8 TK. X DIAMETER	2

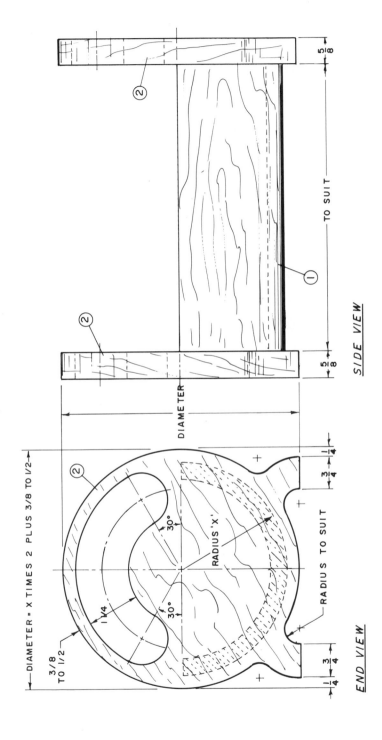

Fig. 9-16. Plans for dough tray: Side and end views.

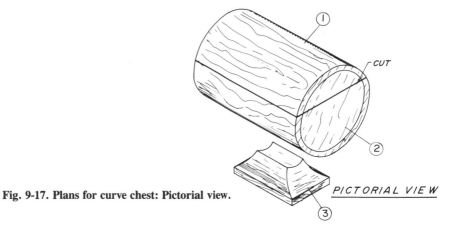

Fig. 9-17. Plans for curve chest: Pictorial view.

PICTORIAL VIEW

Table 9-2. Materials List: Curve Chest.

NO.	NAME	SIZE	REQ'D.
1	SHELL	5 1/2 TO 6 D. X 10 LG	1
2	END	3/8 TK X TO SUIT	2
3	BASE	1 5/8 X 3 - 4 1/2 LG.	1
4	HINGE – BRASS	3/4 X 1 SIZE	1
5	SCREW – FLAT HD.	NO. 8 X 1 1/8 LG.	2

Project 17: Curve Chest

Adding a pedestal on the green cylinder in a horizontal position (Fig. 9-16) gives it the air of a "gift from the Magi."

Use a cylinder from 8 to 10 inches in length. The stock for the ends should be 3/8-inch thick. The base can be an interesting section of scrap wood from another project. Mark cylinder ends by standing the cylinder on edge and marking the circle from the inside. The ends are cut on the band saw, disk sanded to the line, and glued into place. Make sure that the grain of both ends are parallel when glued into place (Fig. 9-17, Table 9-2).

Cut the whole unit open on the band saw. Use a block on each side to prevent the cylinder from rolling. (Rolling can break the band saw blade.) Clearly lay out the cut line on the entire cylinder. Make the cut for the lid all at once. Sand the top and bottom until the fit is smooth and true. To hinge, use 3/4-×-1-inch brass hinges screwed into place.

The base is merely a piece of wood with the curves cut on the band saw, using the rim of a coffee can for a pattern. The top curve that attaches to the cylinder was sanded with the nose of the belt sander. The cylinder is screwed into the base with flat-head screws, from the inside of the chest (Fig. 9-18).

Finish the chest as you wish. Painting and stenciling is very attractive, and the chest may be lined.

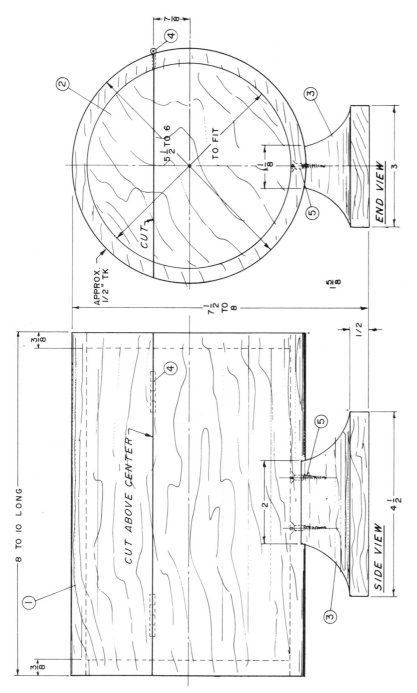

Fig. 9-18. Plans for curve chest: Side and end views.

Project 18: Piggy Bank

Using the cylinder and two blanks that are cut with the band saw to the pattern design, this little piggy will come all the way home in no time (Fig. 9-19).

Make a 5-inch diameter cylinder. Using a drill and $1/8$-inch bit, make the penny slot on the top by drilling consecutive holes to create the opening. Use a chisel and sandpaper to smooth to the appropriate size. Drill a 1-inch hole directly under that slot on the cylinder to accommodate the plug (Table 9-3).

Draw the front pattern onto the $3/4$-$\times$-$6^1/2$-inch square. Using the band saw, cut in and block out the ears and legs first, making them sharper than if you would when following the round cut. Cut the round curve and include all the details around the perky ears and legs.

Using a 1-inch bit, hand drill into the pattern for the nose. Drill two little $3/16$-inch holes for the eyes. Eyes can be cut from dowels, then stained and glued in when gluing the nose in place. The nose and the plug are cut from a 1-inch dowel. Cut the nose $1^1/8$ inch long and the plug 1 inch long. For variety, we stained the nose a different color than the face and body, and included two small drill bit nostrils (Fig. 9-20 and 9-21).

Fig. 9-19. Piggy bank.

Table 9-3. Materials List: Piggy Bank.

NO.	NAME	SIZE	REQ'D.
1	BODY	5" DIA. - 5 LONG	1
2	FRONT	3/4 X 6 1/2 SQUARE	1
3	BACK	3/4 X 6 SQUARE	1
4	NOSE	1" DIA. 1 1/8 LONG	1
5	EYE	3/16 DIA. X 1/4 LONG	2
6	PLUG	1" DIA. X 1" LONG	1

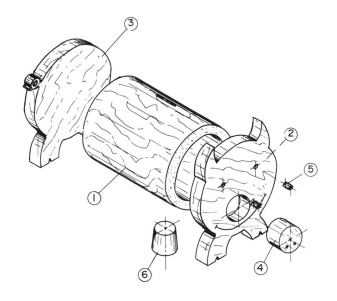

EXPLODED VIEW

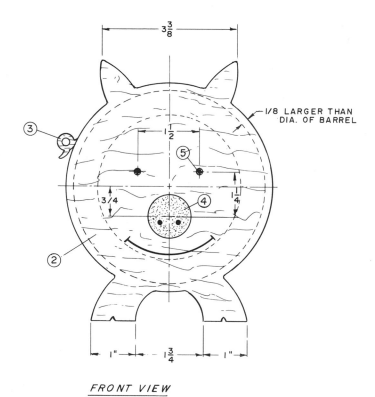

FRONT VIEW

Fig. 9-20. Plans for piggy bank: Exploded and front views.

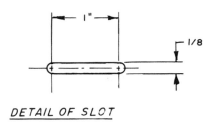

DETAIL OF SLOT

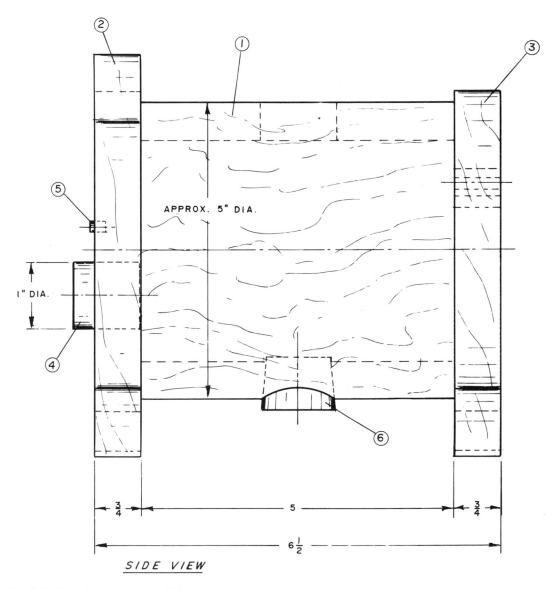

1"

1/8

② ① ③

⑤

APPROX. 5" DIA.

1" DIA.

④

⑥

3/4

5

3/4

6 1/2

SIDE VIEW

Fig. 9-21. Plans for piggy bank: Side view.

Moving to the end, draw the pattern onto the other square. Cut the jaunty tail first to assure clean cutting. Then follow the pattern guide and finish the back on the band saw. Cut the hole in the tail with the same bit used for the slot on top.

You are now ready to assemble your piggy. Place the back piece down on a table. Place wood glue around the circumference of the cylinder bottom, and put the body onto the back piece. Allow to dry. Then bead more glue around the upper end of the body cylinder and attach the front, making sure to stand the bank up and level the pig's feet. Clamp and dry. When dry, glue the nose and eyes into place.

Paint works on this fellow, but I loved the stain effect. Experiment with different colors for a new breed of piggy bank. Painted or stained, this will bring squeals of delight from any penny saver.

Project 19: Round Birdhouse

This little tree apartment for the local winged neighbors is very classy with its salt box roof and cylindrical walls. Use a cylinder with bark to simulate the natural environment of the little feathered friend (Fig. 9-22).

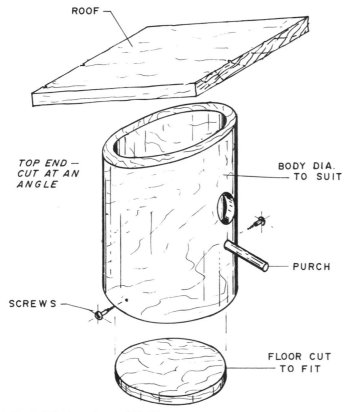

Fig. 9-22. Exploded view of round birdhouse.

To create the salt box roof angle is tricky. It is cut with the band saw, using a block or clamp to a V-block to avoid rolling. Rolling will break the saw blade. It can also be clamped to a table and sawed by hand with a crosscut saw. A chain saw is also a possibility. Just be sure the cylinder is clamped safely in this process as well.

Cedar shakes can be used for a simple and attractive roof. If you can curve the top of the cylinder, you can make yet another type of roof, using another half cylinder. Let your imagination go wild. You can use slab cuts of logs that are sliced at the sides to form a point for the roof.

The bottom of the birdhouse is the clean-out door. It moves on two nails that are diametrically opposed to form a flip door (Fig. 9-23).

The width of the opening for the house is important. Some houses are never occupied because the little renter doesn't like the opening size. Refer to a bird guide for the hole sizes various birds prefer.

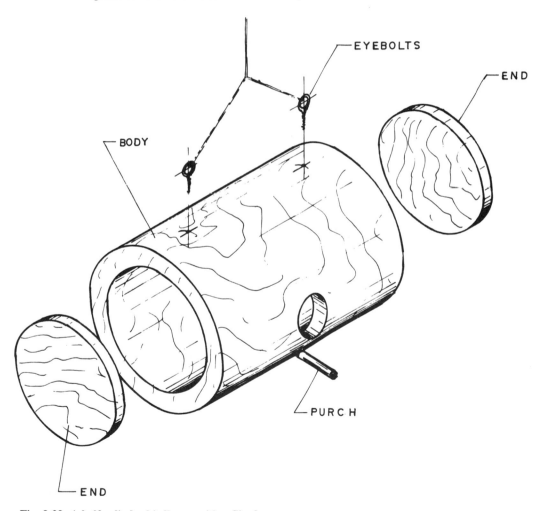

Fig. 9-23. A half-cylinder birdhouse with a flip door.

Project 20: Ornate Plant Holder

This project is simple. The success of the resulting holder depends on a little work from the gardener. After placing a crawling plant into the holder, the leaves must be trellised through the "swiss cheese" holes. Within a few months this plant holder really shows its true beauty. It can also support a potted plant (Fig. 9-24).

Start with a green cylinder. Draw a bottom circle and cut it on the band saw. It should fit loosely on the inside of the cylinder to allow for seasonal changes in the wood. Nail the bottom into the cylinder.

Using a forstner bit on the drill press, randomly drill holes through the sides. Use one size or vary them. Or use the saber saw and make some varying shapes.

If leather straps are to be used in hanging the plant holder, make $1/4$-inch holes in three or four locations around the top of the holder. Poke the leather in place and tie.

These plant holders can also be used to hang a small light, or can even be turned upside down to become a type of lamp. They are not recommended for candles; the fire danger obvious.

Macrame works beautifully with this project. Use the holes for the cord.

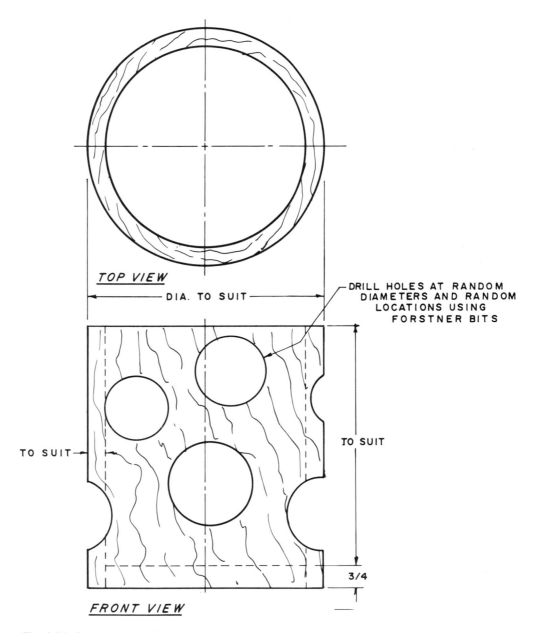

TOP VIEW

DIA. TO SUIT

DRILL HOLES AT RANDOM
DIAMETERS AND RANDOM
LOCATIONS USING
FORSTNER BITS

TO SUIT

TO SUIT

3/4

FRONT VIEW

Fig. 9-24. Ornate plant holder.

III

Router Techniques and Templates

THE ROUTER IS VERY ACCURATE, ESPECIALLY DURING REPEATED OPERATIONS, when used with a template. The template will guide either the router base or the spinning shaft so that the cut may be repeated, again and again, each the same. A well-made template system will last years and save countless hours of layout work. The template will guide the router in machining an edge (straight or curved), routing a pattern in the middle of a blank, cutting a mortise, and a number of other operations.

10
Templates

THE DESIGN AND FABRICATION OF THE TEMPLATE DEPENDS ON THE TASK AND the materials at hand. Template materials are usually chosen for their stability, wear resistance, and cost effectiveness. Templates that will be used again and again over a period of years may justify a great deal of effort and the best materials in their construction. On the other hand, many templates are so specialized that they are discarded after the job. They need only be elaborate enough to ensure their accuracy. Templates can be constructed from materials at hand: plywood, particleboard, plastic, metal, and hardboard. These materials tend to be stable, easy to work with, and readily available.

Shop-built templates are usually cheaper, stronger, more accurate, and more versatile than their manufactured sheet metal cousins. Consider building your own before you buy. Examine over-the-counter router jigs and templates such as circle jigs, letter guides, guide fences, and mortise jigs carefully. They are often very flimsy—poor seconds to shop-built templates. The mirror in the next chapter is made with a shop-built template that guides the router base.

Project 21: Hand Mirror

This attractive hand mirror is cut out in less than three minutes with a router template (Fig. 10-1). It can be sanded and finished within the hour. Once made, the router template system is good for one mirror or one hundred!

The challenge here was to design a jig/template system that would turn out a nearly finished project with the router. The router was to cut the mirror shape,

Fig. 10-1. Hand mirror.

round the corners, and rout a circle to house the mirror. Eventually this was accomplished in three operations. First the mirror indent was routed out, then half the mirror profile cut in the top side. The jig was flipped and the profile cut repeated on the back side. The mirror simply dropped out of the jig (Figs. 10-2 and 10-3).

Two router bits are required for the mirror: a $1/2$-inch mortising bit for the mirror insert and a $3/8$-inch modified roundover bit for the mirror profile. The $3/8$-inch roundover bit can be modified by grinding off the drum on the end of the cutter, or ordered from Amana, bit no. 49704, 1250 Brunswick Ave, Far Rockaway, NY 11691 or call 718-327-6100. This allows the bit to be plunged into the stock and moved around the inside of the template.

Study Fig. 10-4 for construction details. The template jig was originally designed for a round router base measuring $5^7/8$ inches in diameter. Lay out the template patterns according to the diameter of the router base used. The mirror may be cut with one router, changing bits between operations, but it is easier to use two routers if you have them, and not fuss with changing a cutter bit.

Examine the layout plans for the template. Dimensionally stable material such as particleboard, hardboard, or plywood should be used for the template. It is important to cut the template with absolute accuracy: slight deviations in the

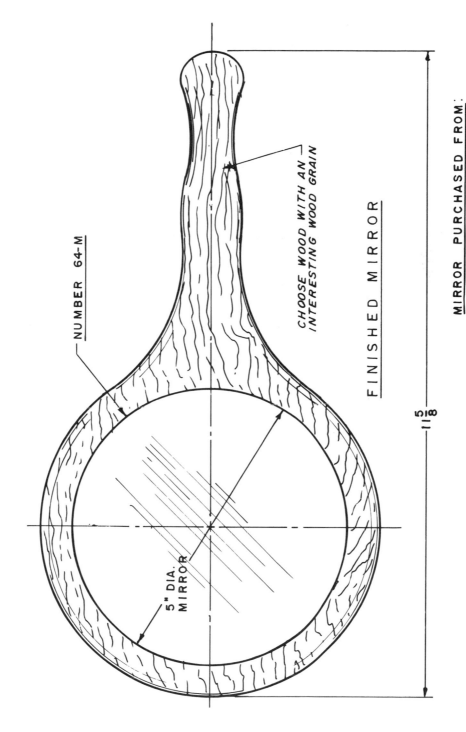

NUMBER 64-M

CHOOSE WOOD WITH AN
INTERESTING WOOD GRAIN

FINISHED MIRROR

5" DIA.
MIRROR

11 5/8

MIRROR PURCHASED FROM:
MEISEL HARDWARE SPECIALTIES
P.O. BOX 70
MOUND, MINNESOTA 55364-0070

Fig. 10-2. Plans for hand mirror: Finished mirror.

179

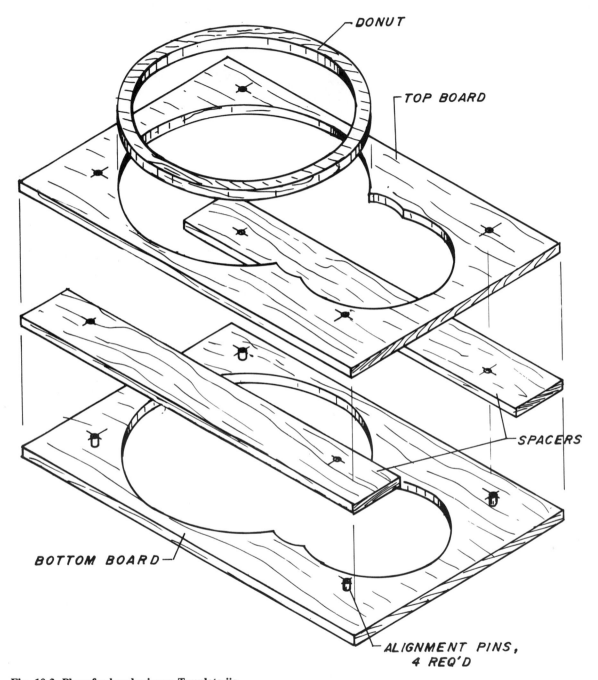

DONUT

TOP BOARD

SPACERS

BOTTOM BOARD

ALIGNMENT PINS,
4 REQ'D

Fig. 10-3. Plans for hand mirror: Template jig.

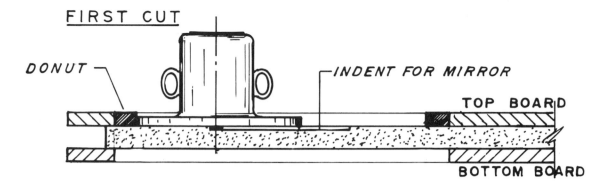

FIRST CUT

DONUT

INDENT FOR MIRROR

TOP BOARD

BOTTOM BOARD

REMOVE DONUT

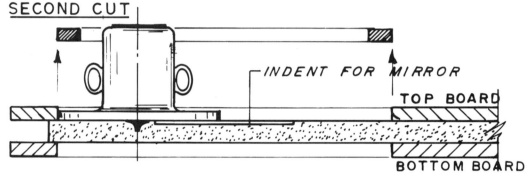

SECOND CUT

INDENT FOR MIRROR

TOP BOARD

BOTTOM BOARD

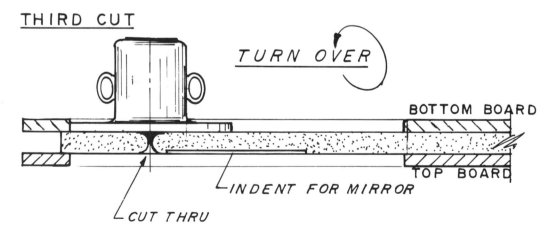

THIRD CUT

TURN OVER

BOTTOM BOARD

TOP BOARD

INDENT FOR MIRROR

CUT THRU

Fig. 10-4. Plans for hand mirror: Routing.

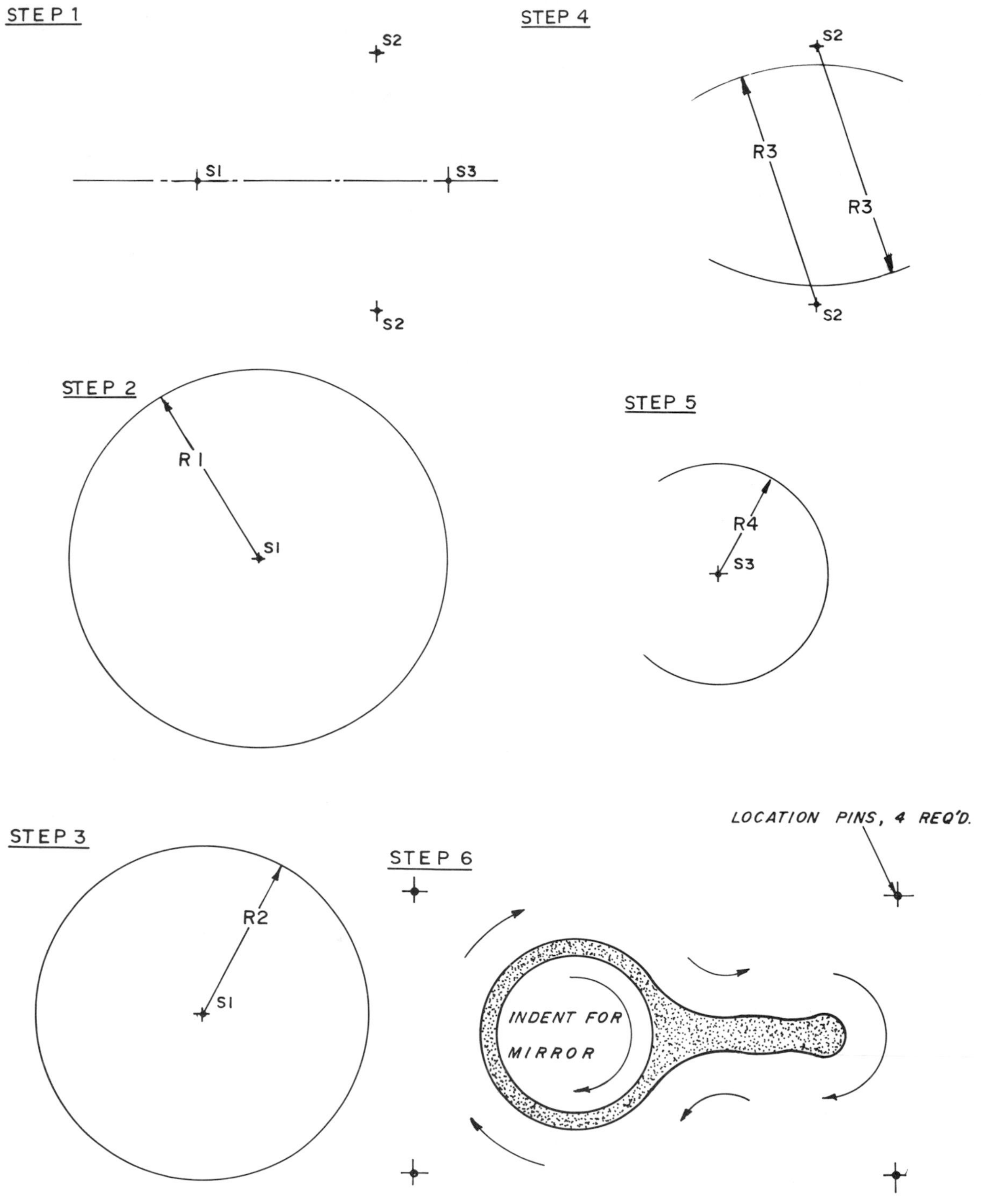

STEP 1

S2

S1   S3

S2

STEP 2

R1

S1

STEP 3

R2

S1

STEP 4

S2

R3

R3

S2

STEP 5

R4

S3

STEP 6

LOCATION PINS, 4 REQ'D.

INDENT FOR MIRROR

Fig. 10-5. Plans for hand mirror: Layout for cutting template.

182

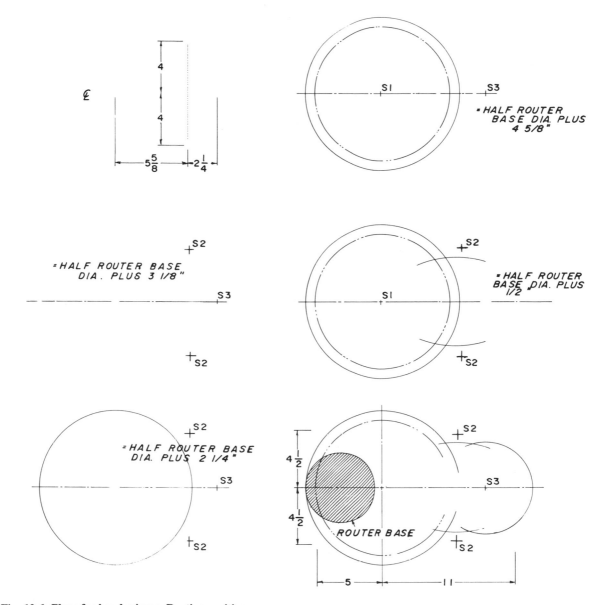

Fig. 10-6. Plans for hand mirror: Routing positions.

template seem to magnify themselves in each mirror and consequently more sanding is required with each mirror.

The pattern will be cut into two identical templates, one for the top of the mirror and one for the bottom. Layout follows these six steps (Figs. 10-5 and 10-6):

1. Locate four circle or arc centers: S1, S2, and S3. All dimensions are in inches.

2. Draw a circle around S1. The radius is half of the router base, plus $3^1/_8$ inches.

3. Draw another circle around S1. The radius is half of the router base, plus $2^1/_4$ inches. This locates the inside of the donut that routs the mirror indent. It is removed when the mirror is cut from the board.

4. Draw two arcs respectively from S2 and S2. The radius is half of the router base, plus $4^5/_8$ inches.

5. Draw a third arc around S3. The radius is half of the router base, plus $^1/_2$ inches.

6. Locate four pin locations that will hold the jig together.

As previously stated, the template cutting must be very accurate. Drill $^1/_4$-inch alignment pin holes, then insert dowels to hold the top and bottom template together. Cut them out together so they remain exactly the same shape. Lacking a scroll saw, I used a band saw to cut the inside shape. I entered on the

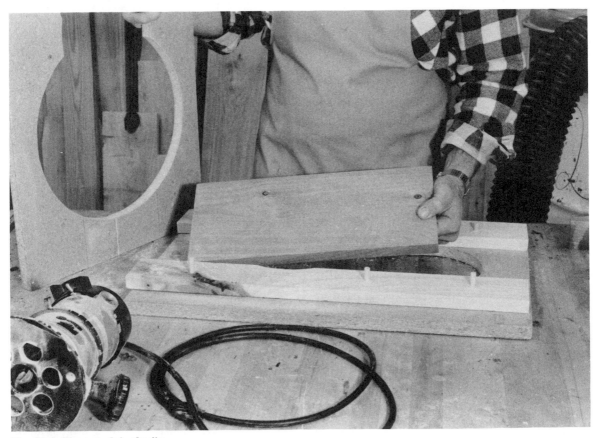

Fig. 10-7. Place stock in the jig.

184

and later inserted veneer into the band saw kerf and glued the template back together.

Cut out the round donut and save it. You will need only one of the two; discard the other. Don't worry if the donut is ruined in this operation, the donut may be cut from other stock and inserted later. Cut to the inside of the lines and sand to the lines later. A drum sander in the drill press works well here. The inside of the donut and the inside of the template should be smooth and symmetrical. The donut may be made to fit tightly in the jig by wrapping masking tape around the rim.

Now cut spacers exactly ³/₄-inch thick to fit between the templates. The spacers will secure the mirror stock in the center of the jig, as well as provide a surface for the router to ride upon.

When cutting multiple mirrors, slide a long board ³/₄-inch thick into the jig (Fig. 10-7) and clamp the assembly to the table. Place the round donut in the jig and rout the mirror insert first (Fig. 10-8). Use a ¹/₂-inch diameter mortising bit for this operation (Fig. 10-9).

Remove the donut and rout one half of the mirror with the router base guided against the inside curves of the template. Move the router clockwise so that it stays against the template during the routing operation (Fig. 10-10).

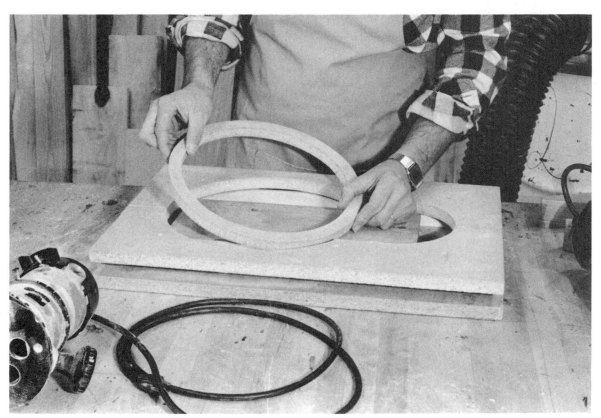

Fig. 10-8. The round donut is used to rout out the mirror insert.

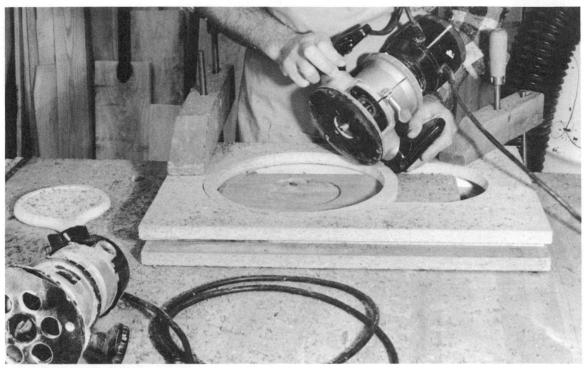

Fig. 10-9. Use a ¹/₂-inch mortising bit to rout out the mirror insert.

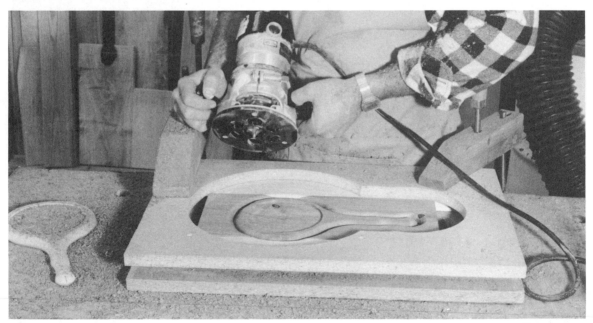

Fig. 10-10. Remove the donut and rout the outside profile of the mirror with a modified ³/₈-inch roundover bit. Move the router clockwise.

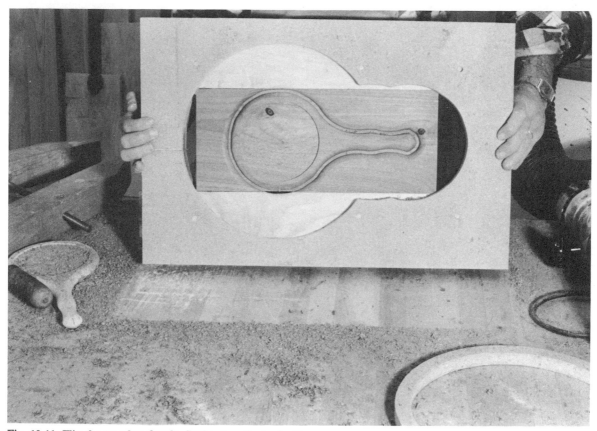

Fig. 10-11. Flip the template for the final cut on the back side.

Next, turn the assembly over and clamp again to the table (Fig. 10-11). Be sure the stock does not slide back or forth in the jig as it is flipped. Make the last cut in the back side of the mirror, again guiding the router clockwise. When the cut is complete, the finished mirror will drop down, away from the cutter (Fig. 10-12). Usually there is a small tang left on the mirror edge, which can be sanded off.

Glue the mirror in after applying the finish. Contact or rubber cement is good for this bond.

Each mirror profile is the same, but variations are possible by varying the wood and finish used. Laminated stripes may be added to the mirror stock, or the entire mirror blank may be comprised of glued laminated stock such as in a cutting board. The texture of the mirror can be changed by sanding or sandblasting. Drill the handle for hanging up or for a leather strap. Paint the mirror glass around the edges or stencil the back of the mirror. These variations in materials, texture, and color will make one mirror completely unlike another, except for shape.

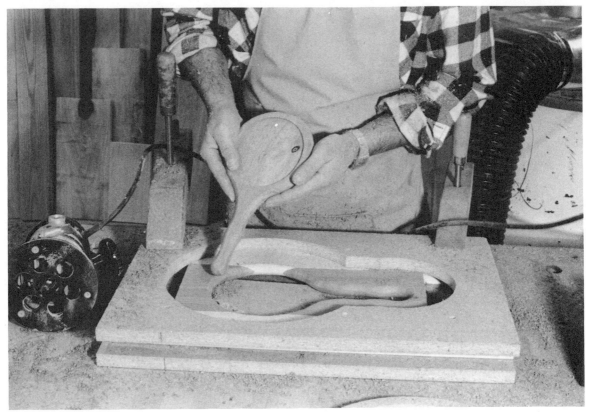

Fig. 10-12. The mirror drops away from the cutter.

11
Double Track Jig

WOODWORKERS ARE ALWAYS SEARCHING FOR THE FOOLPROOF JIG OR FIX-ture. According to my experience, there really is no such thing as "fool-proof." However, a few jigs discovered after trial and error come reasonably close (Fig. 11-1).

One such jig is a double fence router system for cutting dados, rabbets, and sliding dovetails. I believe that a router is the safest way to make these cuts—if the stock is clamped down and both hands are on the router.

The double fence illustrated here is a simple homebuilt jig, easily constructed with scrap stock. This system will guide the router through dados, rabbets, and sliding dovetails without wandering. You won't have to experience that sinking feeling of slipping away from a single fence when working on an expensive part. Alignment is a snap.

Select the first router bit to rout a slot in the end piece of the jig. This slot can be used to line up with the next layout lines. Two router jigs—with $3/8$-inch, $1/2$-inch, $3/4$-inch, and a dovetail in the separate ends of each—will meet most needs. I use one jig with a $3/4$-inch dado in one end and a $1/2$-inch dado in the other to cut nearly all the shelves in my woodworking class, including blind dados.

Begin by cutting rails of straight-grain stock long enough for your needs. The rails will be clamped to the stock, so each rail must be wide enough to allow the router to slide by the clamps without obstruction. Generally rails $3/4 \times 2 \times 24$ inches will do just fine. Cut two end pieces for each jig $3/4 \times 2 \times 10$ inches. The inside edge of the rails and ends must be jointed so they are straight and true.

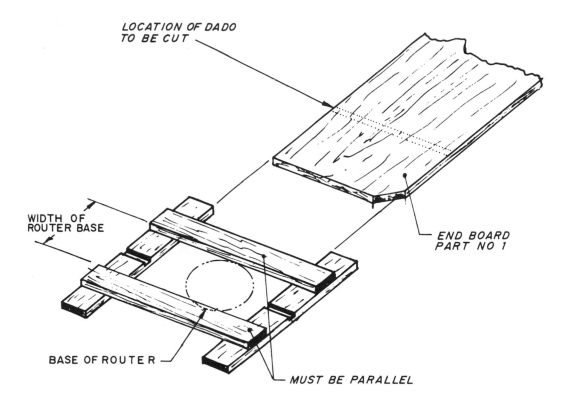

LOCATION OF DADO TO BE CUT

WIDTH OF ROUTER BASE

BASE OF ROUTER

MUST BE PARALLEL

END BOARD PART NO 1

ROUTER FENCE TO MAKE DADOS

Fig. 11-1. Double track jig.

Assemble the jig. Place one rail over the end, and glue and screw the rail exactly 90 degrees to the end piece (check with a framing square). Place the router base on the end piece to locate the second rail. Repeat the process for the other end. The rails should be tight enough to the router base to keep it from wandering, yet not bind the router anywhere along its path.

Place the jig on the stock to be machined, with the end placed firmly against the edge of the stock. Clamp both to the workbench. If the jig is new, the first pass with the router will cut the end piece of the jig. If the cut is not 90 degrees to the stock, a shim between the end piece and the stock will ensure proper alignment. If the cut is on or near the edge of the stock (such as for a rabbet), place material that is the same thickness under the second rail to provide support for the router.

When machining stock that is less than the 3/4-inch thickness of the end piece, place scrap under the workpiece, or simply slide the end piece of the jig off the edge of the workbench. This will make a tight fit when clamping. Deep or wide cuts will require several passes of the router, increasing the depth at each pass.

Fig. 11-2. Sliding bookrack.

Project 22: Sliding Bookrack

If you love to read, here is the perfect project (Fig. 11-2). The rack expands with the newly acquired volumes, yet won't lean and fall—the ends slide into each other with sliding dovetail joints.

The base parts are cut from ³/₄-inch stock, the ends from ⁵/₈-inch stock. The finished dimension will be 10³/₄ inches, with the slide having a 5¹/₄-inch to 6-inch expansion. Follow the bill of materials to cut the parts to size (Table 11-1). The dovetail slide is made with a horizontally or vertically mounted router. The dados for the end parts are machined on the table saw, and the heart-shaped design is cut with a saber or scroll saw (Fig. 11-3).

Here are a few tricks to make the construction of the bookrack easier: Before the sliding dovetail is machined, glue one end base (part 2) to the end grain of part 1. When the dovetails are cut in the base, the end base will be cut as well. Crosscut the end base from the base, then machine the slides (part 4) to fit the base and glue them in place.

Now glue the opposite end base (part 2) to the base (part 1). Cut the dados in both end bases to house the ends of the bookrack. One is attached to the base and the other to the slides, so that they can be held safely on the table saw with the miter gauge (Fig. 11-4).

Using the plans, cut the curves in the upper edges of the ends (part 3) at 1-inch radius. Locate and draw the heart design. Calculate the radial centers for drilling. Using the drill press method, drill out the tops of the heart. Finish the job with the jigsaw or router.

Put the ends into the end base and use flat-head wood screws (No. 8, 1³/₄-inch long) to join the pieces. Use felt padding over the screw heads to prevent any furniture damage.

Table 11-1. Materials List: Sliding Bookrack.

NO.	NAME	SIZE	REQ'D.
I	BASE	3/4 X 6 - 10 3/4 LG.	I
2	END—BASE	3/4 X 1 1/8 - 6 LONG	2
3	END	5/8 X 5 1/4 - 6 L.G.	2
4	SLIDE	3/8 X 2 - 11 7/8 LG.	2
5	SCREW- FLAT HD.	NO. 8 - 1 3/4 LONG	4
6	FELT PAD	1/2 DIA.	4

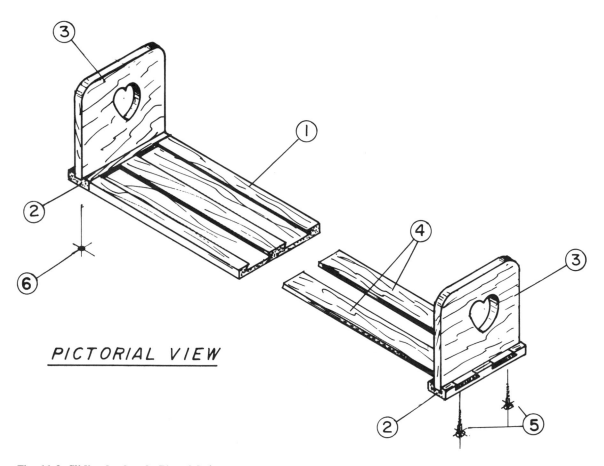

PICTORIAL VIEW

Fig. 11-3. Sliding bookrack: Pictorial view.

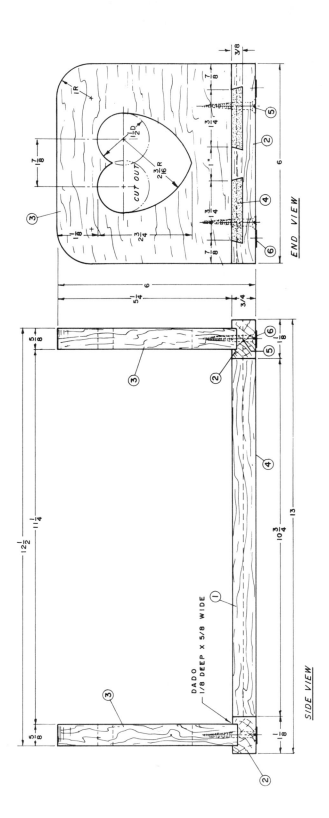

Fig. 11-4. Sliding bookrack: Side and end views.

193

Project 23: Contemporary Bookshelf

This bold Scandinavian book/display shelf made of red oak is a full 48 inches long and 42 inches high (Fig. 11-5). It was designed to fit a 4-foot module system. Standing alone it is simple and functional, and an ideal weekend project for the beginning to intermediate woodworker. It could easily be made in lengths less than those illustrated, in order to fit specific wall space.

Solid red oak was chosen because it was one of the strongest native woods available. The unsupported span of the shelf—nearly 4 feet—requires a strong wood to keep the shelf from sagging under a full load of books. If the shelf is kept at 4 feet, use oak or another strong wood. Weaker woods may be used for shorter shelves. Clear white pine, for example, should not be used in shelf spans exceeding 30 inches. Lower grade large-knot pine may only be used for spans less than 24 inches.

Fig. 11-5. Contemporary bookshelf.

Table 11-2. Materials List: Contemporary Bookshelf.

NO	NAME	SIZE	REQ'D.
1	END	3/4 X 8 1/2 – 42 LONG	2
2	SHELF	3/4 X 8 1/2 – 47 LONG	4
3	BACK BOARD	3/4 X 4 – 47 3/4 LG.	1
4	KICK BOARD	3/4 X 3 – 46 1/2 LG	1
5	SCREW-FLAT HEAD	NO. 8 – 1 1/2 LONG	30
6	PLUG – WOOD	SIZE TO SUIT	30
7	PLUG – SCREW	1/2 DIA. – 5/8 LONG	16

The 3/4-inch-thick shelf parts may be purchased already surfaced on four sides, and all the same width, for convenience. Or you might want to machine the parts to size, which is more economical (Table 11-2).

Glued-up boards are also acceptable, and in my opinion, as strong or stronger than solid stock. I use dowels occasionally to help align stock when gluing edge to edge, although the dowels are not necessary for strength. Apply glue to the edge of the boards, but not on the dowels nor in the dowel holes. The dowels, if glued across the grain, restrict wood movement in high or low humidity. The integrity of the glued joint is dependent upon tight-fitting edges and quality glue. Edges should fit tightly together without light showing through. Yellow glue (alphatic resin) is a great adhesive but it is not designed to fill gaps from poorly jointed edges. Select grain patterns carefully and joint the edges well, and glue lines will be just about invisible (Fig. 11-6).

No matter how straight the boards are jointed and how carefully they are ripped, they never seem to end up exactly the same width when the shelf is assembled. This is because few boards are really flat when ripped on the table saw. Boards that are cupped mysteriously become slightly wider when they are forced flat in the dado joint. Don't worry, light hand planing will trim the wide board down after assembly. Before ripping, however, check cupped boards by placing them on a flat surface with the cup up. Press down on the crown and see if the board will flatten. If it flattens with the push of a hand, it can be forced into the dado later. If the board shows signs of cracking or is difficult to flatten, it should be ripped down the middle, with one half flipped end for end and reglued.

Rip the back board and kick board to width after the ends and shelves. The combined width of both the kick board and the back board is cut from one shelf-size board so there is a minimum of waste (Fig. 11-7).

The radial arm saw is the best tool to cut the parts to length. Once the radial arm saw is adjusted and checked so that it cuts square, it may be easily set up for multiple operations. Set the saw up to square one end of each shelf, then slide the shelf to the other side of the table for the second cut. Use a stop block clamped to the radial arm saw fence on the second cut, so that all shelves are exactly the same length. In three settings the cutting is finished. The shelves (part 2) are cut at 47 inches, the kick board (part 4) at 46½ inches, and the ends (part 1) at 42

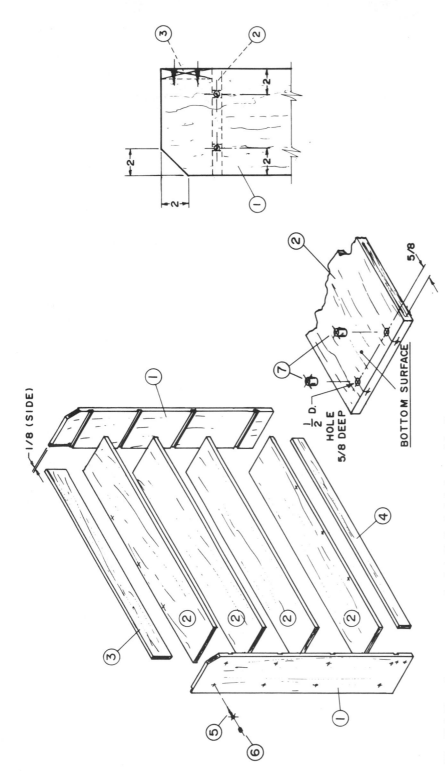

Fig. 11-6. Plans for contemporary bookshelf: Exploded view and details.

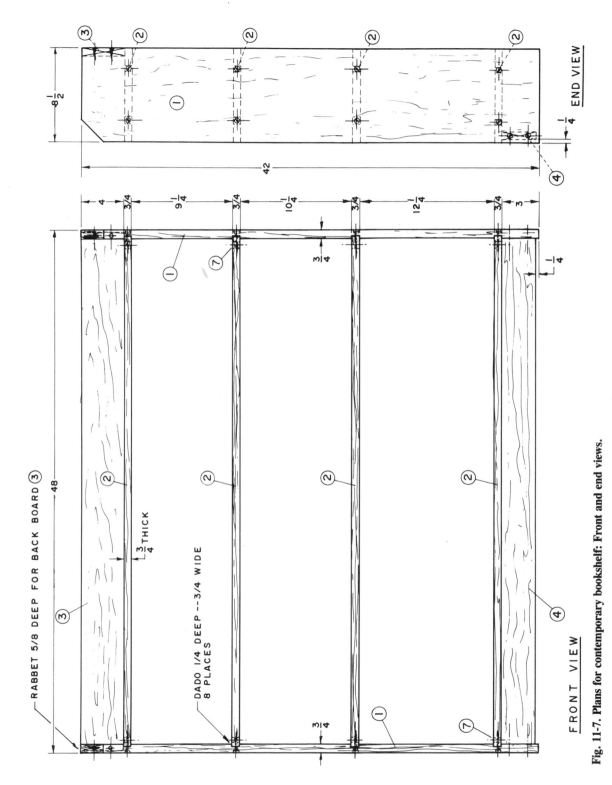

RABBET 5/8 DEEP FOR BACK BOARD ③

DADO 1/4 DEEP --3/4 WIDE
8 PLACES

$\frac{3}{4}$ THICK

FRONT VIEW

END VIEW

Fig. 11-7. Plans for contemporary bookshelf: Front and end views.

197

inches. Leave the back board long, and cut it to finish length after the sides and shelves are assembled. Check to be sure the corresponding parts are square and the same length.

Next, lay out the dado locations in the end parts (part 1). Although the dados may be cut by hand, or with dado blades on the table or radial arm saw, I prefer the router for this operation. A 3/4-inch dado bit will leave a clean, flat-bottomed cut that is ready to be glued and assembled. The router, coupled with a simple homemade jig, is safer and more accurate than other methods. Another plus is the router's ability to follow the contour of a slightly cupped end board. The dado remains the same depth across the entire width. Keeping the dados consistently at 1/4-inch depth across a slightly cupped end board will allow the board to be pulled flat against the end grain of the shelf during assembly.

Clamp a simple double-track jig to the end boards to guide the router so it does not wander during the cutting operation. Cutting the dados is a safe, accurate, and easy operation with the double fence guiding the router and both hands on the router handles. Take a few minutes to make the jig, and it will serve well in many future projects. Use it to cut dados, rabbets, and sliding dovetails.

After the dados and rabbets are finished, cut the top front angle of each board. Check the shelf fit in the dados. If they are tight at this point, sand the end surface of each shelf lightly so as not to decrease the thickness of the shelf board. The dados should fit snugly. A trick to aid in assembling the shelves, especially those that are cupped, is to sand slight rounds on the end grain of the shelves, except where they show at the edges. This will help the shelves slide into snug dados during assembly (Fig. 11-8).

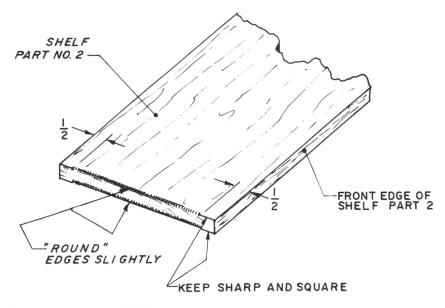

ENDS OF SHELVES

Fig. 11-8. Ends of shelves.

Screws and glue are used to hold the bookcase together. Screws, however, don't hold as well in end grain as in side grain. Dowels can be inserted into the shelves to provide more bite for the screws. Insert the dowels in holes drilled into the bottom of the shelves at screw locations. This provides a strong grip for the screw and the dowel doesn't show from the top. A flat-bottomed bit is needed for this operation. Alternatively, you might want the dowel to show from the top. If it is of contrasting wood or color, it is an interesting design feature. Lay out all drill locations in both the end boards and shelves accurately before drilling.

Countersink the holes in the end boards so that plugs may be used to hide the screwheads. The countersunk hole should remain shallow so that the screw head has plenty of wood underneath it, even though wood is removed for the dados on the other side.

Sand or plane all parts prior to assembly. Next, lay masking tape down on both sides of the dados in the end boards. The tape will protect parts from glue that squeezes out during assembly.

The easiest way to assemble the shelves is on a wide bench with the shelves and end boards on edge. A power screwdriver and a separate drill is very handy. Glue all the dados in one end board, then insert the shelves and secure them, one at a time. After each shelf is inserted in the dado, predrill in the shelf end grain by drilling through the countersunk holes that are already drilled in the end boards. Then drive the screws with the power screwdriver. Do the same on the second side, but don't drive the screws completely home until all the shelves are put into the dados. Shelves that are not flat may be clamped flat with a wide wooden screw clamp to help fit in the dado.

As soon as the second side is in place, check the squareness of the case. Measure across the diagonals from opposite corners on the face of the bookcase. If the diagonals do not measure the same the case is out of square. Square the case with a bar clamp across the end boards of the bookcase. Place the bar clamp in the same direction as the longest diagonal, snugged up until the diagonals measure the same. Protect the bookcase with scrap wood so the bar clamp doesn't do damage to the wood surface.

When the case is square, insert the top brace and kick board and screw in place. The kick board is designed not to touch the floor. The small gap left beneath the kick board will keep the bookcase resting square on the end boards in case there would be a slight hump in the floor.

Remove the masking tape after assembly. Cut plugs for the screw holes and glue in place, with the grain of the plug following the grain in the end boards. Careful selection of plugs by color and grain will make the plug practically invisible after sanding and finishing. Let the plugs stand above the finished surface. Later, sand, file, or shave the plugs to the finished surface. Then finish sand.

The bookcase illustrated was finished with four coats of Watco Golden Oak oil finish, each applied one day apart. The third and fourth coats were wisk-sanded smooth with 360 sandpaper, then given a coat of wax. Periodically the bookcase is polished with furniture polish.

12

Horizontal Router

NEED TO MAKE A MORTISE-AND-TENON JOINT? WANT A SLIDING DOVETAIL, OR box, or rabbet? Try horizontal routing. The horizontal router is a natural for these joints and more. This section includes plans for a home-built horizontal router table (Fig. 12-1).

Horizontal routing makes good sense when cutting molding and machining joint work. Routers are mounted vertically in a router table to mimic the shaper arrangement, and hence duplicate the shaper's functions at competitive cost. However, for the majority of arrangements a side-mounted router is superior. The horizontal router table has two large table surfaces, vertical and horizontal. This convenient arrangement makes it easy to rout molding profiles with stock held flat or up on edge.

The machine is especially at home with mortises and sliding dovetails. Frequently, I choose a sliding dovetail to join table rails to their legs. With the horizontal router, this takes only minutes per table. Box joints, rabbets, and plow grooves are quick, clean, and accurate with this home-built machine (Fig. 12-2).

Horizontal routing machines may be purchased on the retail market. Strong Industries manufactures one, called the Jointmatic. This is a rugged and accurate machine that elevates the bit (vertical table) above the table 8 inches using an excellent crank system that is calibrated at $1/16$ inch per rotation.

So much of our shop work necessitated the use of the Jointmatic that I became intriqued with developing a shop-built machine that measured up to the versatility and efficiency of the Jointmatic at a fraction of the cost.

Fig. 12-1. Horizontal router.

Project 24:
Horizontal Router Table

This shop-built machine was to mount a router on a vertical surface—adjustable up and down—against a flat, horizontal table. In addition, it had to include clamping arrangements for jigs and fixtures. After some thought, I placed other restrictions on the development of the machine. It should be simple in construction, no frills, and constructed of materials readily available in the wood shop (Fig. 12-3).

With these things in mind, I discarded some of my wilder designs. In the end I settled on mounting the router on a rotating disk that is essentially clamped to the edge of the machine table. As the disk is rotated, the router bit is adjusted in an arc, up and down. The bit may be rotated down on the left or right hand side of the table to allow maximum table length before the bit or after, depending on the operation. Height is indexed in the rim of the disk, and read at table height. A sturdy clamping bar keeps the disk tightly against the base. The base is a simple

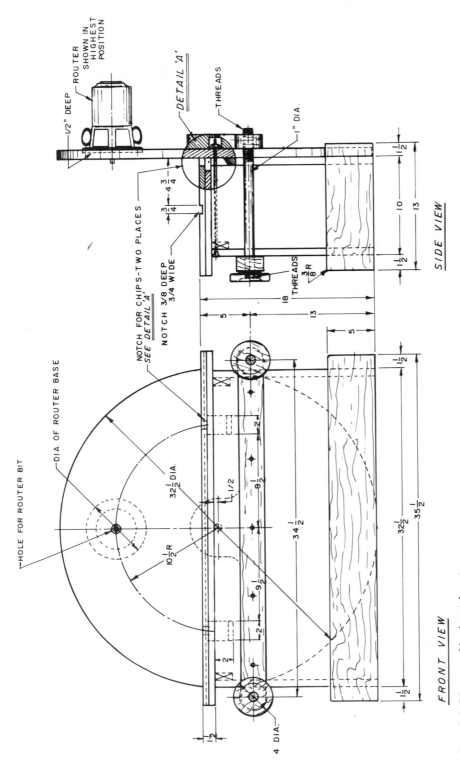

Fig. 12-2. Diagram of horizontal router.

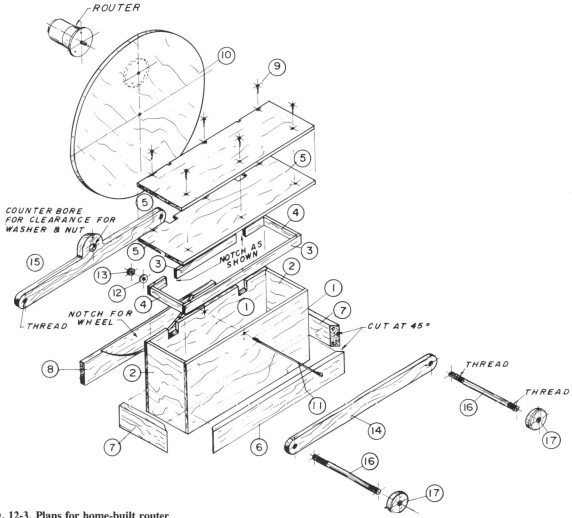

ROUTER

COUNTER BORE
FOR CLEARANCE FOR
WASHER & NUT

NOTCH AS
SHOWN

NOTCH FOR
WHEEL

THREAD

CUT AT 45°

THREAD

THREAD

Fig. 12-3. Plans for home-built router.

box filled with sand to dampen vibrations and stabilize the machine. The table surface projects 2 inches over the front and sides of the machine to provide clamping surface for jigs and fixtures.

Particleboard covered with plastic laminate provides a stable hard surface for the disk, table, and base. Most of the materials came from rejected countertop material, which kept the cost down. Provisions may be made to attach a vacuum hose to the base to pull chips away from the cutter head.

The plans and text included here illustrate the machine at its simplest. The bit adjusts from below table surface to 8 inches above. If you choose to alter the plans for materials at hand, remember that the accuracy of the machine is dependent on the flatness of the disk and table surface, and they must be exactly 90 degrees to one another.

Table 12-1. Materials List: Home-Built Router.

NO	NAME	SIZE	REQ'D.
1	FRONT / BACK	3/4 X 16 1/2 – 32 1/2	2
2	END	3/4 X 8 1/2 – 16 1/2 LG.	2
3	TOP SUPPORT	3/4 X 2 – 31 LG.	2
4	TOP SUPPORT	3/4 X 2 – 7 LG.	2
5	TABLE	3/4 X 12 – 36 LG.	2
6	BASE – FRONT	1 1/2 X 5 – 35 1/2 LG.	1
7	BASE – END	1 1/2 X 5 – 11 1/2 LG.	2
8	BASE – REAR	1 1/2 X 5 – 35 1/2 LG.	1
9	SCREW – FLAT HEAD	NO. 8 – 3" LONG	6
10	WHEEL	3/4 X 32 1/2	1
11	WHEEL AXLE	3/8 DIA. 12" LONG	1
12	WASHER	3/8 SIZE	1
13	NUT – HEX	3/8 DIA.	2
14	LOCK BAR FRONT	1 1/2 X 3 – 37 1/2 LG.	1
15	LOCK BAR REAR	1 1/2 X 8 – 37 1/2 LG.	1
16	LOCK SHAFT	1" DIA. X 15 LG.	2
17	LOCK WHEEL	1" X 4 DIA.	2

Start by constructing the base. Cut parts 1, 2, 3, 4 listed in the bill of materials (Table 12-1). Use particleboard or 3/4-inch plywood. Assembly with drywall screws and a screw gun speeds up this step. Use glue in all joints. Notice the plans do not include a bottom in the box; the bottom is optional. A lightweight machine that may be transported needs no bottom; the chips simply fall through the bottom. If the machine is stationary, or if a vacuum hose is to be attached, include a bottom.

Figure 12-4 illustrates one example. Here the machine is stationary and sand is added to the base to resist vibration. The box is also baffled to keep the sand from shifting. During the assembly of the base it is important that the top of the box be exactly 90 degrees to the back of the box. Figure 12-5 shows this angle checked with one of the table boards temporarily screwed in place.

Now cut and laminate the disk. Figure 12-6 shows the jigsaw used to cut a disk that has been laminated. The laminate may also be glued on the surface after the disk is cut out and trimmed with a router and bit designed for the purpose. Laminate both sides of the disk; this will keep it flat. The edge of the disk is laminated as well, because it provides a good surface to index the machine. Locate the center of the disk and drill a 3/8-inch hole for the wheel axle.

Locate the router position and countersink the router base halfway through the back of the disk. It is, of course, best to mount a permanent router on the machine. If one is not available, purchase an extra router base for the machine.

Fig. 12-4. The horizontal router base with optional bottom and base filled with sand for stability.

Fig. 12-5. The router table must be square with the back of the machine.

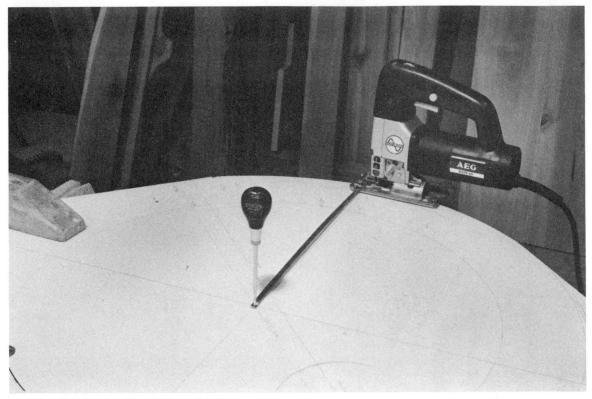

Fig. 12-6. The disk is cut out with a saber saw.

An extra base will allow the router to be used for other things and be quickly remounted to the horizontal router. The size or horse power of the router chosen is not so important as the construction of the collet chuck. Many light-duty collet chucks allow the bit to slip, heat, and work out. Choose a router with a rugged chuck.

Figure 12-7 illustrates a jig used to guide a router into the back side of the disk. The circle fits the base of the router that was installed. Unscrew the plastic laminate from the base of the router and use these threaded holes to attach the router base to the machine with flat-head machine screws countersunk from the front of the disk.

Drill holes in the machine box for the axle bolt, then bolt the disk to the back of the box. Be sure that both holes are in line and square to the back of the box. Use a washer and two nuts so the nuts will not work loose as the disk is rotated. Cut and install the base parts 6, 7, and 8. The rear base part is notched to allow clearance for the disk.

Cut both lock bars from hardwood (parts 14 and 15). The front lock bar is screwed to the machine box. The rear lock bar is hung over the wheel axle nut and pulled toward the front with threaded dowels and hand wheels. This prevents the disk from rotating during each cut. If threading tools are not available,

Fig. 12-7. A router with template is used to cut the insert for the router base in the disk.

threaded steel rod may be substituted and metal nuts epoxied in countersunk holes drilled in the rear lock bar (Fig. 12-8).

Next, cut and glue together the table parts (5). The table is glued up and laminated before it is installed. The six screws holding the table to the machine are countersunk from the top surface of the machine. For this reason, they may be removed and the table surface shimmed square with the disk, if necessary. Locate the screws away from possible contact with the router bit as the disk is rotated into the table on the left and right.

Rout the miter gauge slot in the table surface after the top is installed. The slot is $3/4$-inch wide and deep enough to house the miter gauge "borrowed" from the table saw. Cut the slot through the laminate with a carbide bit, making several passes. Do this by clamping a straightedge against the face of the disk. The slot must be parallel to the disk face and far enough away from the disk to allow the metal head of the miter gauge to pass safely by the router cutters.

Calibrating the center height of the cutters is the final step. Install a V bit in the router for these steps.

Figure 12-9 illustrates the horizontal router marked at each $1/4$ inch of height. Rotate the disk to align the center of the V bit at table height, then index the edge of the disk with a sharp knife. Continue rotating the bit upward and

Fig. 12-8. The lock bar across the back of the disk is clamped with wooden dowels and threads.

Fig. 12-9. The height to the center of the bit is indexed on the side of the disk.

marking at least every $1/4$ inch. As the bit is rotated higher, the marks will become farther apart. (The scale is not linear.) The accuracy of this step is important when box joints are cut with the horizontal router.

Project 25: Jointwork

Figure 12-10 illustrates common jointwork from the horizontal router table. The router bit may be adjusted in two ways: The bit may be raised or lowered by rotating and locking the disk, and the bit depth may be controlled by adjusting the router base.

Mortises are cut by plunging stock into the mortising bit and moving the stock to the left. Feed from left to right if the bit is plunged, or if the bit is safely under the stock. (Cut from the underside.) Cut the tenon with the same bit, extended the same distance from the disk, but lowered to remove stock from the underside. Each pass is guided with the miter gauge. Flip the stock to cut the other three sides of the tenon. Round the corners of the tenon with a file to fit into the mortise.

Fig. 12-10. The horizontal router easily cuts these joints.

Sliding dovetails are easy on the horizontal router. First, set the depth of the dovetail bit and rout the dovetail recess. Then lower the bit and rout the dovetail. This is done by cutting below the stock, flipping the stock, and routing the other side. Slowly elevate the bit until the parts fit. The 45-degree miter jig (Fig. 12-11) is made to cut the dovetail bracket.

Box joints require careful indexing of the disk. The sequence shown here is for 1/4-inch box joints. The box joints may be made from any width dado bit, provided the disk is indexed to the width of the bit. The horizontal router illustrated was indexed every 1/4 inch on the disk rim and is perfect for 1/4-inch box joints.

Start by setting the depth of the bit slightly greater than the thickness of the stock. Lower the bit to the zero degree point and cut part A. Screw a board to the miter gauge so that both parts of the joint (A and B) are supported during the cut. This will keep the back of the joint from chipping out. After part A is cut, raise the bit to 1/4 inch and cut part B. Then raise the bit to 1/2 inch and cut part A (Fig. 12-12).

Repeat this, working up the joint until finished. Raise the cutter 1/4 inch between cuts and switch the parts between each cut (Figs. 12-13 and 12-14).

Fig. 12-11. A 45-degree miter jig is made to cut the dovetail brackets in.

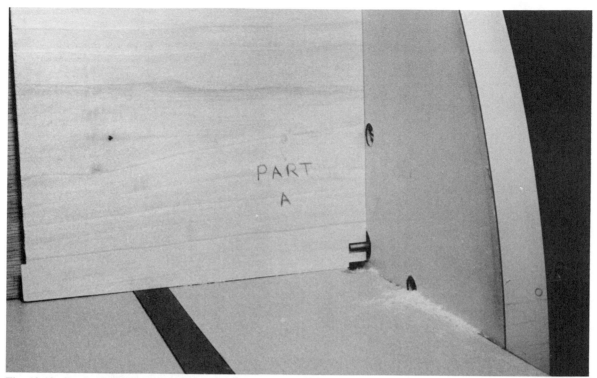

Fig. 12-12. Cutting box joints (part 1).

Fig. 12-12. Cutting box joints (part 2).

Fig. 12-14. The box joint is complete.

Clean rabbets, dados, and a host of other joints are made by installing the right cutter and moving the stock across the table from right to left. Stop blocks and other jigs may be clamped to the table to guide specialized cuts. It is always best to make light cuts with repeated passes. Heavy cuts will bog the router down and ruin accuracy.

IV
Drill Press Techniques

Project 26: Corner Shelf

T HIS KNOCKDOWN CORNER SHELF OF POPLAR AND BIRCH DOWELS IS HANDY IN any corner (Fig. IV-1). The arrangement is quite elementary, very versatile, and can be made in one evening. These simple shelves are adjustable for objects including dolls, dishes, plants, and tools. The dados underneath each shelf fit onto dowels in the side parts. Side parts, which look like ladders, are supported by the corner of the room (Figs. IV-2 and IV-3).

Fig. IV-1. Corner shelf.

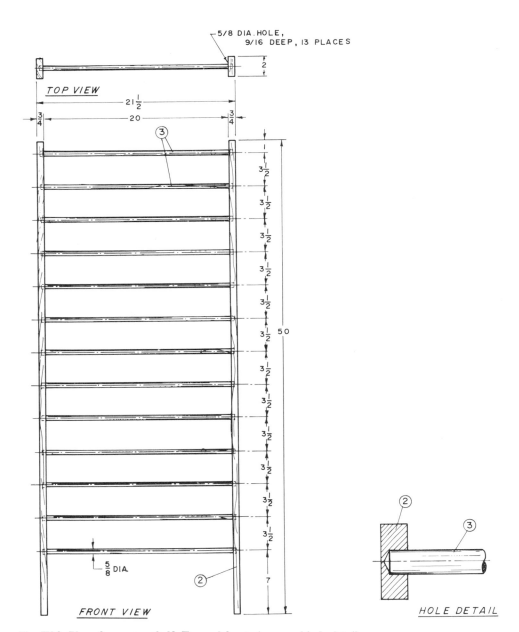

Fig. IV-2. Plans for corner shelf: Top and front views, and hole detail.

Table IV-1. Materials List: Corner Shelf.

NO.	NAME	SIZE	REQ'D.
1	SHELF	3/4 X 14 – 34 LG.	4
2	RAIL	3/4 X 2 – 50 LONG	4
3	DOWEL	5/8 DIA. – 21 1/8 LG.	26

215

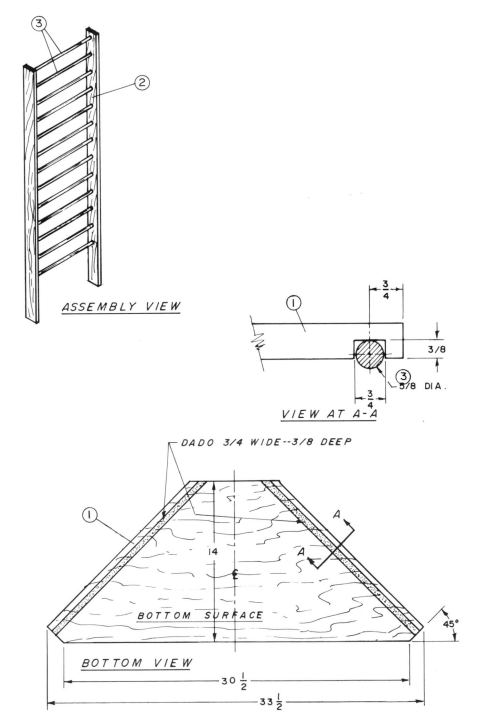

ASSEMBLY VIEW

③

②

VIEW AT A-A

①

3/4

3/8

③

5/8 DIA.

3/4

DADO 3/4 WIDE--3/8 DEEP

①

A

A

14

¢

BOTTOM SURFACE

BOTTOM VIEW

45°

30 1/2

33 1/2

Fig. IV-3. Plans for corner shelf: Assembly and bottom views.

The corner shelf will require construction of a simple jig to use with the drill press. It is called a drill spacer jig.

Begin by constructing the two ladder sides. Cut the rails and dowels to length (Table IV-1). The hole locations in the rails need not be laid out; the jig will space them automatically (Fig. IV-4).

The jig is simply four pieces of wood with a short section of $5/8$-inch dowel used as a stop. This section of dowel will index the rail holes from the top. Use scrap stock and follow Fig. IV-5 for construction details. The jig has three hole locations in the top. The first locates where the $5/8$-inch drill from the drill press quill is centered. Thus, the jig may be removed from the drill press table and quickly remounted for future use. The second hole is 1 inch from the first, and the third hole is $3^1/2$ inches from the first.

Fig. IV-4. The drill spacer jig. The hole close to the drill is used once, to start each rail.

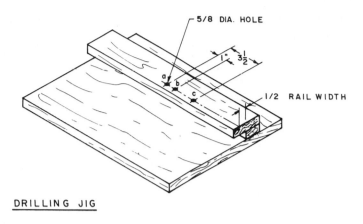

5/8 DIA. HOLE

1" 3½

a
b
c

1/2 RAIL WIDTH

DRILLING JIG

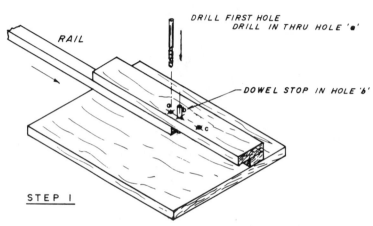

RAIL

DRILL FIRST HOLE
DRILL IN THRU HOLE 'a'

DOWEL STOP IN HOLE 'b'

a
c

STEP 1

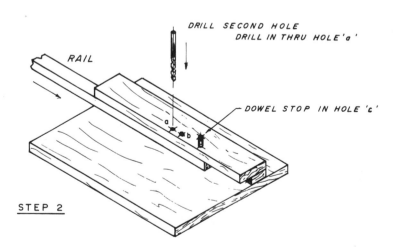

DRILL SECOND HOLE
DRILL IN THRU HOLE 'a'

RAIL

DOWEL STOP IN HOLE 'c'

a
b

STEP 2

Fig. IV-5. Steps for drilling with a drill press and jig.

Fig. IV-6. The second hole is used to index all other holes in each rail.

Clamp the jig to the drill press table, the first hole lined up with the ⁵/₈-inch drill. Adjust the drill depth to penetrate ⁹/₁₆ inch into the rail. A flat-bottomed forstner bit is best for this operation. Place the short index dowel in the second hole and slide the rail in the jig until it is stopped by the index dowel. Drill the first hole, then move the index dowel to the third hole. Slide the rail to the right until the index dowel drops into the hole that was just drilled. Drill, raise the index dowel, and slide the rail down until the index dowel drops into the hole just drilled. Repeat this until all 13 holes are drilled. Repeat for the other rails (Fig. IV-6).

Glue and clamp the sides of the shelf together. Check for squareness before the assembly is left to dry.

Shelves may be cut from one 14-inch wide board or glued panel. Lay out the shelves "flip-flop" on the board so there will be little waste. Cut with the radial arm saw. Set ⁵/₈-inch wide dado blades in the table saw and cut the dados using the fence as guide.

Sanding and finishing are next. These corner shelves were oiled with Watco natural oil finish. Urethane would be better for a durable, wear-resistant finish.

Appendix
Suppliers

THESE COMPANIES SELL WOODWORKING PRODUCTS TO WOODWORKERS AND also carry a line of woodworking books to sell.

Tremont Nail Co.
21 Elm St., P.O. Box 111
Wareham, MA 02571

The Brass Tree
308 N. Main St.
Charles, MO 63301

Garrett Wade Co. Inc.
161 Avenue of the Americas
New York, NY 10013

Bob Morgan Woodworking Supplies
1123 Bardstown Rd.
Louisville, KY 40204

Brookstone Co.
Vose Farm Rd.
Peterborough, NH 03458

Constantine
2050 Eastchester Rd.
Bronx, NY 10461

Cryder Creek Wood Shoppe, Inc.
Box 19
Whitesville, NY 14897

The Fine Tool Shops
20 Backus Ave. P.O. Box 1262
Danbury, CT 06810

Leichtung Inc.
4944 Commerce Pkwy.
Cleveland, OH 44128

Meisel Hardware Specialties
P.O. Box 70
Mounol, MN 55364-0070

Silvo Hardware Co.
2205 Richmond St.
Philadelphia, PA 19125

Trendlines
375 Beacham St.
Chelsea, MA 02150

Woodcraft
41 Atlantic Ave. P.O. Box 4000
Woburn, MA 01888

The Woodworkers Store
21801 Industrial Blvd.
Rogers, MN 55374

Woodworkers Supply of New Mexico
5604 Alameda, N.E.
Albuquerque, NM 87113

Index

Index

Other Bestsellers of Related Interest

HOME WIRING FROM START TO FINISH
—Robert W. Wood

This is a do-it-yourselfer's manual on installing and repairing electrical wiring. Using this guide, you can safely and successfully wire an entire residence. More than 421 two-color illustrations and photographs appear throughout the book, making it easy to identify components and follow Wood's step-by-step directions. It's a good introductory text for anyone interested in pursuing an electrican's license. For personal wiring jobs in your own home, this guide will make sure you pass inspection every time. 272 pages, 421 illustrations. Book No. 3262, $17.95 paperback, $26.95 hardcover

MASTERING HOUSEHOLD ELECTRICAL WIRING—2nd Edition—James L. Kittle
"An excellent fix-up book for the homeowner."
                                            —Pejepscot (Maine) Cryer

Update dangerously old wiring in your house. Add an outdoor dusk-to-dawn light. Repair a malfunctioning thermostat and add an automatic setback. You can do all this and more—easily and safely—for much less than the cost of having a professional do it for you! 304 pages, 273 illustrations. Book No. 2987, $16.95 paperback only

AIR CONDITIONING AND REFRIGERATION REPAIR—2nd Edition—Roger A. Fischer and Ken Chernoff

The second edition of *Air Conditioning and Refrigeration Repair* covers the basics of electricity, refrigeration theory, controls, refrigerants, water chemistry, soldering, and charging the units, as well as the latest developments in the field itself. The authors explain in a nontechnical manner the features, care, and repair of all components of a refrigeration unit. 384 pages, 229 illustrations. Book No. 2881, $18.95 paperback only

BASIC BLUEPRINT READING—John A. Nelson

With the knowledge gained from this book, you will become expert at reading not only mechanical drawings, but construction, electrical, and plumbing drawings as well. Using a step-by-step approach, John Nelson incorporates the latest ANSI drafting standards as he covers all aspects of blueprint reading. Through straightforward language and excellent example illustrations, Nelson shows you how to identify and understand one-view, multi-view, sectional-view, and auxiliary-view drawings. 256 pages, 235 illustrations. Book No. 3273, $19.95 paperback, $28.95 hardcover

FROM RAMSHACKLE TO RESALE: Fixing Up Old Houses for Profit—Carol Boyle

This book includes extensive guidelines showing you how to identify properties that can be recycled quickly and inexpensively. With no experience, little cash, and this book, you can successfully convert an eyesore into an asset. Using the expert instruction provided, you will confidently progress through the stages of inspector, electrician, plumber, painter, carpenter, and interior designer to real estate broker. 304 pages, 192 illustrations. Book No. 3162, $15.95 paperback, $24.95 hardcover

HOME ELECTRICAL WIRING MADE EASY: Common Projects and Repairs—Robert Wood
"Written for people with no more electrical expertise than changing light bulbs, this book presents safe and easy procedures."   *—Popular Electronics*

Following Wood's step-by-step instruction, you will become a master at installation, repair, and replacement of outlets, three- and four-way switches and timers, ceiling lights and fans, automatic garage door controls, thermostats, 220-volt appliance outlets, door bells, outdoor lighting, and more. 208 pages, 190 illustrations. Book No. 3072, $16.95 paperback only

BUILDER'S ESTIMATING DATABOOK
—Robert L. Taylor and S. Blackwell Duncan

This book is composed of more than 600 invaluable tables that enable you to estimate at a glance the quantities of materials you need for any building project—right down to the last nail. It is the most complete, concise, and easy-to-use book ever compiled for general use. A professional reference for architects, builders, engineers, designers, contractors, home manufacturers, and to do-it-yourselfers, the authors provide answers to nearly every building question imaginable. 410 pages, 577 illustrations. Book No. 2768, $17.95 paperback, $26.95 hardcover

DREAM HOMES: 66 Plans to Make Your Dreams Come True—Jerold L. Axelrod

If you are planning—or just dreaming—of building a new home, you will find this book completely fascinating. Compiled by a well-known architect whose home designs have been featured regularly in syndicated "House of the Week" and *Home* magazine, this beautifully bound volume presents one of the finest collections of luxury home designs ever assembled in a single volume! 86 pages, 201 illustrations. Book No. 2829, $16.95 paperback only

INCREASE ITS WORTH: 101 Ways to Maximize the Value of Your House—Jonathan Erickson

"an idea book, filled with sensible advice on what makes a home valuable." **—San Francisco Examiner**

The author profiles the three basic types of home buyers, defines the factors that affect resale value, explains two basic methods of determining your home's resale value, and shows you what rooms play the biggest role in deciding the value of a home. 208 pages, 105 illustrations. Book No. 3073, $14.95 paperback, $23.95 hardcover

KEEP ITS WORTH: Solving the Most Common Building Problems—Joseph V. Scaduto and Michael J. Scaduto

This book outlines how to identify, remedy, and prevent the building problems home owners are most often concerned about; wet basements, roof leaks, decay and wood-boring insects, energy maintenance, maintaining mechanical systems, and other home building hazards. 304 pages, 271 illustrations. Book No. 2961, $16.95 paperback, $25.95 hardcover

MIKE McCLINTOCK'S HOME SENSE CARE AND REPAIR ALMANAC—Mike McClintock

This is the owner's manual that should come with every house. McClintock is well known for his magazine and newspaper columns, radio program, and guest appearances on television talk shows, where he obliges his audiences with straight talk about home maintenance, improvement, remodeling, and repair. In this comprehensive guide, he supplies a compendium of time and money-saving advice, and tips on a variety of home-ownership topics. 480 pages, illustrated. Book No. 3149, 19.95 paperback only

WHOLE HOUSE REMODELING GUIDE —S. Blackwell Duncan

This book features hundreds of remodeling, renovating, and redecorating options described and illustrated step-by-step! Focusing on interior modeling, the possibilities that exist for floors, windows, doors, walls, and ceilings are comprehensively explored. Complete detailed, illustrated instructions for projects are easy to follow. 448 pages, illustrated. Book No. 3281, $19.95 paperback, $28.95 hardcover